REFLECTIONS
TO INSPIRE & CHALLENGE

THIS
NEW DAY

PATRICK JURD

COVENTRY
PRESS

Published in Australia by
Coventry Press
33 Scoresby Road
Bayswater Vic. 3153
Australia

ISBN 9780648804499

Copyright © Patrick Jurd 2020

Cataloguing-in-Publication entry is available from the National
Library of Australia http://catalogue.nla.gov.au/.

Cover design by Ian James - www.jgd.com.au
Cover photograph by Patrick Jurd
Text design by Megan Low (Film Shot Graphics FSG)
Set in Vollkorn

Printed in Australia

CONTENTS

Foreword 5

Introduction. 7

January 11

February. 37

March 61

April. 85

May. 109

June. 133

July 155

August 177

September. 199

October 221

November 247

December. 269

For AnneMaree – my everything

All proceeds from the sale of this book will be donated to St Maria Mazzarello Secondary School, Venilale, Timor-Leste and sent via Salesian Missions Australia.

FOREWORD

There is a passage, attributed to Abba Poemen, from the period of 'desert spirituality' in the fourth century:

The nature of water is soft, that of stone is hard...

But if a bottle is hung above the stone, allowing the water to fall drop by drop, it wears away the stone. So it is with the word of God; it is soft and our heart is hard, but the one who hears the word of God often, opens the heart in awe of God.

The reflections in *This New Day* illuminate three essentials contained in these words. First, they invite us into an organic process of lived spirituality in the stuff of our lives. Patrick leads us to 'the Word' that shapes our heart in the day-to-day, here and now. Secondly, the reflections are centred in and soften the heart. 'The heart' in ancient times was not disconnected from 'the head' – it was the mysterious space of wholeness within us, holding together the different dimensions of the self. Patrick's words allow us to enter into this space gently and wisely. Thirdly, the reflections open us - 'to awe' – that generative place within us from which springs new possibilities and growth. These new possibilities are the gift of Patrick's affirming, challenging and ultimately transformative reflections. This wonderful book will be of great value for personal prayer and in leading others; and I encourage you to let it speak and open the heart.

Christopher Morris
Catholic Theological College, Melbourne

INTRODUCTION

I have been writing reflections for about ten years. I did not intend to start. It is something that just *happened*. Of course, another way of looking at that is that I allowed myself to be guided by the Holy Spirit. Or, in a Franciscan frame, I discovered a talent that had been placed there by God and put it to use. Part of this talent is expressing myself in a very positive, encouraging way.

I was talking with my darling wife, AnneMaree, about putting together another book of reflections, along the lines of the three that have already been published, *To Strengthen and Encourage, Always in God's Presence* and *Guided into the Truth*. She demurred and instead suggested that I compile a set of reflections for each day of the year. Also, that these daily reflections are intended for everyone, rather than the focus on working with young people like my previous books. While I didn't take to the idea immediately, I have learnt to trust my wife's take on matters and here we are.

So, *This New Day* is intended for someone to open at a particular date and be inspired. Their inspiration could begin with the passages from scripture, Franciscan or Lasallian writings. If we are open, scripture always has something to say to us. My reflection is *my* take on the scriptural passage and is also intended to inspire. There is space for you to jot *your* take on scripture underneath each reflection. This book also includes my writings on God's creation, in its many forms. Consequently, I write from my observation of the passage of the seasons. Those in the Northern Hemisphere will need to flip winter and summer and so on.

Which brings us to the title of the book. It is easy to allow ourselves to be burdened by our responsibilities or our worries. Each day is a gift and we constantly need to remember that fact. Thus it is our responsibility to make the most of the present – treating it as such, by *being* present and treating it as the extraordinary gift that it is. This gift is brought into sharper focus in a time of pandemic.

May you appreciate this day and your giftedness.
Wishing you peace and all good.

Patrick Jurd

May 2020

As a teacher I have been influenced by two charisms.

John Baptist De La Salle founded the Brothers of the Christian Schools in France around 1680. He has been proclaimed the patron saint of Christian educators and was ahead of his times in so many ways. He emphasised the relational nature of teaching: 'you are engaged in a ministry wherein you are required to touch the hearts of those entrusted to your care'. The Lasallian charism is alive around the world in a variety of ministries.

Helene de Chappotin also known by her religious name, Blessed Mary of the Passion, founded the Franciscan Missionaries of Mary in the late 19th century. The FMMs began Ave Maria College, where I work, in 1963. The FMMs are one shoot of the Franciscan family which, from its birth in Assisi through St Francis and St Clare in the early 13th century, has spread throughout the world.

JANUARY

1 January

A New Year
Arrives
And I have a choice.

Will I make the most of
This year's blessings
And challenges?

Will I be
A person of integrity
And practise what I preach?

Will I be motivated
By love
Or fear?

2 January

See, I am making all things new. (Revelation 21:5)

Perhaps you can relate when I find I can be burdened by the past. I can relive old hurts. I can beat myself up about old mistakes. Things that I can do nothing about – except learn the lesson and not repeat my mistake. What better at the start of a new year than to retain the lessons but leave the past behind. I know that each new day has its own challenges but I also know that each day has its blessings if I am alert. Despite the seeming similarity of each day I need to become aware and awake to the differences. No two sunrises or sunsets are identical. I'm living/working with the same people – but what's happening for them? Amidst the similarities, recognise and celebrate blessings and differences of this new day.

3 January

*When Jesus realised that they were about to come
and take him by force to make him king, he withdrew
again to the mountain by himself. (John 6:15)*

Clearly, Jesus does not subscribe to the dictum 'no publicity is bad publicity'. As he says later in John's Gospel, his 'kingdom is not of this world'. He eschews personal fame because he is doing his Father's will and works. Jesus' antidote to the lure of fame is to seek solitude – inferring that he would pray. This passage makes me wonder, 'how often do I turn to prayer?' and 'how easily am I seduced by fame?'

4 January

Brilliant blue sky
Radiating warmth
Soaked up
By the trees
And humans
Aware
Or not
Of this tableau
In its power
Simplicity
Aglow with God's love
Of creation

5 January

People came to Jesus from everywhere. (Mark 1:45)

We are searching – searching for wholeness, searching for truth. As Augustine said: 'Our hearts are restless until they rest in you'. Compassion and integrity such as Jesus displayed are attractive. They speak to us on a very deep level: 'you have the words of eternal life' (John 6:68). They resonate with us. You can be yourself, know you're accepted and that there are no hidden agendas. When I find some answers, some truth, whatever its form, I will return to that truth I've found. So I will continue to pray and/or marry that person and/or put down roots in that community so that I grasp that portion of my truth.

6 January

The stone rejected by the builders has become the cornerstone. (Psalm 118)

Psalm 118 was written in the context of the fledgling nation of Israel fighting and defeating surrounding nations. This passage is used in Christianity to refer to Jesus. Jesus was not favourably received by the Jewish establishment yet he is pivotal to our faith. This passage may ring true for some readers in the context of their lives: feeling rejected or an 'outsider' but with determination and faith go on to play their part, one that is significant to them.

7 January

O you who answer prayer! (Psalm 65:2)

Addressing God in this way speaks of faith and hope. We believe that prayer is answered. Our experience can be that prayer may not always be answered in the way that we originally wanted it to be. In hindsight, we might glimpse God's plan for ourselves and others. Thus our experience can help us to grow in faith, hope and trust.

With the Holy Spirit at work in us, we journey closer to the faith, hope and trust of the psalmist.

8 January

Warm day
With time
To savour it
The freedom
And sense of relaxation
Heightened
Due to time with friends and
Because I'm with my love

Our world can be so focused
On doing
Which is why it's important
To let go
And just be

9 January

The Lord encourages those who are losing hope.
(Sirach 17:24)

This passage presumes that the person has *not* lost hope and is still open, despite their difficulties. Such encouragement can take a variety of forms. It can be the right word at the right time that buoys a person. It might be a smile. It could be consolation while at prayer. It could be hearing a particular passage of Scripture. It could be wise counsel from a trusted friend. We all want our problems to disappear. But it is enough to be granted the grace to see this moment, or this day, through.

10 January

Do not fear, only believe. (Mark 5:36)

In this passage, Jesus raises the girl from the dead. There are many facets to this story but one view is that in telling them 'do not fear', Jesus is saying to them 'do not look on the surface'. Believing gives us a broader, deeper vision; seeing things as they might be – not just as they are. Believing in this way gives us the grace and strength to deal with difficulties, seeing the situation and people as they might be – living in justice and right relationships.

11 January

The Lord by wisdom founded the earth. (Proverbs 3:19)

Despite what some may say, there is wisdom at the basis of God's creation. It is neither haphazard nor random. The eyes of faith allow us to see this. But the more that science explores creation, the more that the wisdom behind it becomes apparent. The extraordinary and delicate connections of ecosystems are but one example. The infinite subtleties of the vast reaches of space, the electromagnetic spectrum and subatomic particles are others. Importantly, there is a point and purpose to our existence and our relationships. Much like the other areas mentioned, we can choose to build or destroy. Each day, may we marvel at and savour God's creation.

12 January

Jesus said to them, 'Give to the emperor the things
that are the emperor's, and to God the things that are
God's'. (Mark 12:17)

It's so easy to miss the big picture. Our lives can be made
up of so many small tasks and activities, and we can be
so caught up in 'getting them right'. Since God loved
each of us into life, giving 'God the things that are God's'
means giving God our whole heart and mind and soul
– not externals. Or as Andre Cirino OFM puts it, God
placed the gifts, talents and goodness in each one of us
and it is our task to discover and develop that goodness
using it to build community and offer it back to God.

13 January

Blessed be the Lord,
who daily bears us up;
God is our salvation. (Psalm 68:19)

We believe that God is always with us. When life is a
struggle, we can cry to God about our difficulties. Are we
sufficiently open-hearted to be aware of the seemingly-
hidden graces that are present each day, each moment of
our lives? As Shakespeare said, there's the rub. Whether
in joy or difficulty, God is with us. One perspective
upon 'God is our salvation' is that, since God is present
in everyone and everything, we need each person, each
relationship to enrich us and save us.

14 January

God tempts no one. But one is tempted by one's own desire, being lured and enticed by it. (James 1:13-14)

Humans can seek to deflect the blame of an action or situation – what I have heard referred to as 'deny, blame, justify'. Who better to blame than God? 'God made me this way.' One problem with this is that there is no place for free will – what about *my* choices? I do not believe in a God who is a master puppeteer.

Whatever my desires are – for food, for intimacy – it is how we channel those desires. We need food to survive. Yet, when we over-eat, is there some other emptiness we are trying to fill? We each crave for intimacy. There are many ways this can be sated. We are made in the image of God who is love. This is why we are most satisfied in relationships where there is mutual giving and receiving of love.

15 January

Grow up in one place
Live in another
Work here
Work there
Visit plenty of other places
What does it mean
To feel at home?

So subjective
It can be about
A place
Or the presence
Of certain people

Dislocation
Discomfort
Can help some people
Or make others feel
'All at sea'

The truth
As is frequently the case
Lies within

If I am enough
Then so will my world be

Are you at home
Today?

16 January

No one is good but God alone. (Mark 10:18)

At first read, this passage can sound negative but we need to know the context of Mark's Gospel – the persecution by Emperor Nero – so there are fewer 'frills'. Beginning with the creation accounts in Genesis, God's creation is good. Thus the statement, thoroughly Franciscan, that God is the source of all good. As believers and humans we can be caught in a tension. We are each capable of great goodness – love, compassion, selfless giving. But we do not live like that all of the time – at least I know I don't!

It is healthy to regularly give thanks for God's goodness in our world – in ourselves, in others and the panoply of delights in God's creation. And may we ensure that when we extend compassion towards others, there is some compassion left for ourselves and our own failings. Maybe even a measure of humour: 'there I go again!'

17 January

Give, and it will be given to you. A good measure,
pressed down, shaken together, running over, will be
put into your lap; for the measure you give will be the
measure you get back. (Luke 6:38)

As human beings made in the image of our triune God, we are made for love. We find our happiness, our true selves, when we give ourselves away in love, just as we were each loved into life. It is easy, even sensible, to hold back – especially to hold back on forgiveness, the context of this passage. My truth is that the more aware I become of my failings, the more likely I am to forgive others for their failings.

Our world encourages judgment of others. Much of our media is full of it. By trying to be compassionate and forgive others, we help others but also ourselves. We journey towards wholeness and holiness and we bring God's reign just a little closer.

18 January

Then Peter came and said to him, 'Lord, if another member of the church sins against me, how often should I forgive? As many as seven times?' Jesus said to him, 'Not seven times, but, I tell you, seventy times seven'. (Matthew 18:21-22)

The Gospels do not portray Peter as always getting it right. Then, as now, forgiveness can be an issue. Peter has heard Jesus and so knows the importance of forgiving. His answer? The 'perfect' number of seven (numerology was a big deal at the time). Jesus blows that away with an open-hearted forgiveness unlike anything the apostles have witnessed.

A life lesson is the importance of forgiveness to the one doing the forgiving. If we hold on to past hurts, they can be like lead weights on our being and can affect us both spiritually and physically. The open-hearted forgiveness of which Jesus speaks liberates everyone and allows each of us to grow because Love has the space to do its work – turning our hearts of stone into hearts of flesh.

19 January

For the Lord takes pleasure in his people;
he adorns the humble with victory. (Psalm 149:5)

As adults we revel when the young people in our care shine. This is but a reflection of God's joy in her children. We are made to shine. We are made to discover our gifts and use them. The use of our gifts is most fruitful when we build our community with them. We also know that not *only* the humble win – whether in sport, politics or some other endeavour – but it sits best with those who are humble. The champion Roger Federer springs to mind.

20 January

Bartimaeus, son of Timaeus, a blind beggar, was
sitting by the roadside. When he heard that it was
Jesus of Nazareth, he began to shout out and say,
'Jesus, Son of David, have mercy on me!' (Mark
10:46-47)

This healing story leans on ideas of Jesus as a Davidic messiah who will bring mercy and justice – healing the blind. But what of the name – 'son of Timaeus (i.e. *fear*)'? What are the ways in which our fears blind us? Fear blinds us from seeing the everyday good around us. Fear blinds us from seeing the needs of others – we are caught up in our own perceived problems. Fear stops us from being our true, full selves – our fears have us looking over our shoulder in case we made a mistake, rather than celebrating this moment.

Fears hold us back and we need to be liberated… from ourselves. Faith can be a way where we become freed to be our true selves. God's love, reflected through our family and friends, can free us from our fears so that we can see the fears for what they are – the shadows of love.

21 January

Herod said, 'John I beheaded; but who is this about whom I hear such things?' And he kept trying to see Jesus. (Luke 9:9)

One of the themes of Luke's Gospel is about the overturning of power. Herod killed John since people were paying him too much attention. Then along comes Jesus who is attracting even more people. The reader is prompted to ask: who is really in control? Luke's answer: God. Maybe Herod couldn't see Jesus because he was more focused on power than faith.

In our lives, we can 'try to see Jesus' – thinking this is another thing we can control. When we let go of power and control and live our lives with an open-handed faith, we will see Jesus every day – and realise that it is only our perception that has shifted.

22 January

Crashing down
In silent waves
Setting buildings aglow
Making the haze visible
Helping plants
Continue their timeless march
Thus ensuring animals
Can breathe
Giving warmth
Wanted or not
Lighting our way
Brother Sun at work

23 January

The apostles said to the Lord, 'Increase our faith'.
(Luke 17:6)

The Gospels speak of the apostles and they are portrayed as fallible human beings. I suspect many of us recognise that cry to 'increase my faith'. I may think that my faith needs increasing because I do not feel that I'm up to the challenges that I must deal with. I may think my faith needs increasing due to doubts I am experiencing. I may think my faith needs increasing so that I can let go of my control. Then I can pray wholeheartedly 'your will be done'.

24 January

For the Son of Man came to seek out and to save the lost. (Luke 19:10)

Read in its context, this verse continues one of the themes of Luke's Gospel – caring for those 'on the outside'. It is vital that as a church we continue that ministry today so that we can help make the body of Christ whole. Those who are lost have much to teach those whose lives are safe and comfortable – both about humility and faith.

As much as we need to go out to others in need, it's in our best interests to extend compassion to those parts of ourselves that are 'lost'. Whether it is due to a death, changed life circumstances, addiction or the like, we can each feel 'lost'. Such compassion towards ourselves will guide us towards wholeness... and holiness.

25 January

New morning
Fresh
Washed clean
Air filled
With the sound of
Seagulls and
Civilisation
Beetling away
Bright sunshine
Crowns the scene

I can see
Clouds brooding over
The heads of
Botany Bay
Gateway to the
Tasman Sea
And more

The timelessness of
Sand
Sea and
Sky
Yet another time
One that connects to me
Reels me in.
A monument to the First Fleet
Is on the foreshore

Showing
William Douglas and
Mary Groves
My ancestors

The gift of this scene?
The many facets of
Connection
Which is another way
Of describing
God

26 January

... always carrying in the body the death of Jesus, so that the life of Jesus may also be made visible in our bodies. (2 Corinthians 4:10)

Standing up for those in need, for integrity, for truth, can be a hazardous business. We have seen this in people such as Oscar Romero and Dorothy Day. In smaller ways in our own lives, we know that there can be a physical, emotional and psychological cost for being true to our faith. Also, it is more than what I endure; the body also refers to the Christian and Catholic community. 'The life of Jesus' is one of faith, hope, healing compassion and love. Such a life builds community.

This is not easy to live. There are strong societal forces that emphasise the individual as well as personal freedom. Freedom like happiness can be misconstrued. Those societal forces can define freedom in terms of being free to consume. Rather, 'the life of Jesus' promotes community and happiness for the individual as they contribute to 'something bigger than themselves'.

27 January

... be examples to the flock. (1 Peter 5:3)

Whoever I am, someone is looking up to me. I can be an influence – for good or otherwise. In using the language of the passage, Peter asks us to be caring and considerate. Then, as now, each 'sheep' is important. So, in the mundane reality of our lives, it also means there will be times when we need to put our personal needs aside to care for others.

And so we return to integrity. If I am a person of faith, how will others know? It is vital that others see me living my faith in a practical sense – by speaking and acting for justice for the needy in our world. In an everyday sense, people ought to be able to see in me, however partial, a reflection of Jesus. Helene de Chappotin, founder of the Franciscan Missionaries of Mary said to 'walk as a living Gospel' – that people will read the Gospel in us. What will they read in me?

28 January

... the only thing that counts is faith working through love. (Galatians 5:6)

As humans, we want to know 'how to do it' – how to live a life of faith. However, it is easy to be caught up in form or process: 'am I doing it right?' Paul clarifies matters for us: 'faith working through love'. This is simple and clear but it seems to me that it requires us to pay attention to the motives behind our actions. Is *this* action motivated by faith and done in a self-sacrificing way? Or am I acting to ease my own discomfort? Or am I being controlling?

Such close discernment tells us 'how to do it' – in a way that is best for others *and* ourselves, bringing a greater appreciation of God's presence among us.

29 January

Summer bursts
From the flowering gum
With its vivid red blooms
Some sharing their bounty fully
Others in the process of revelation
Tantalisingly filled with nectar
As the bees do their symbiotic part
In this cycle of birth
And re-birth
All augmented by the lorikeet's
Flash of colour.
A similar dance
Is repeated with the grevillea
With different moves

This sacramental moment
Breaks my day open
And widens my eyes
In joy and wonder

30 *January*

And if people were amazed at the power and workings
of nature, let them perceive from them how much
more powerful is the one who formed them. (Wisdom
13:4)

Study of nature whether it is soil, plants, insects, animals, birds, fish, rocks, fossils or so many other 'ologies' – provides us with so many intricate details, so much order, so much richness that I believe the first and most appropriate response is awe. I note that awe is one of the traditional gifts of the Holy Spirit. That awe can inspire us to want to learn more – and appreciate the area of study as something precious and wondrous.

We should remember that God is the author of the Book of Scripture *and* the Book of Nature. As we journey through life, may curiosity, wonder and awe grow at the extraordinary richness and connections in God's creation. But as the quote from scripture reminds us, we must honour the giver of all these precious gifts – by doing our part to take care of them.

31 January

The angel of the Lord came a second time, touched
Elijah, and said, 'Get up and eat, otherwise the
journey will be too much for you'. (1 Kings 19:7)

Life has its struggles that we cannot ignore. What is
important but sometimes forgotten is the need to
nourish ourselves through the difficult times – to not
just 'grin and bear it'. So what nourishes you? It might
be music, art or nature. As people of faith it is in our best
interests to allow those or similar experiences to draw
us closer to God, to see things straight – to give us food
for the journey.

We believe that Jesus is present in the Eucharist –
in the congregation, in God's word, in the priest and
the bread and wine. Thus, we need to remember the
enduring 'food for the journey'.

FEBRUARY

1 February

Grace upon grace
Rain down on us
Or come onto our path
Day after day

The gift of sharing
A laugh
Or another's joy
Or sorrow

The absence of pain
Or fear
Or guilt
Or worry

A sense of belonging
Being at home
Feeling appreciated
Loved

The revelation
That lies within
Our feelings
The wonder in each
Of our senses

The grace to see
The nuance of another

Beautiful sunrise
Or sunset
The shaft
Or glow
Or gleam
Of sunlight
The gobsmacking wonder
Of plants,
Animals,
Our world

May we have
The eyes to see
And appreciate
Our blessings
Every day

2 *February*

*Moses did not know that the skin of his face shone
because he had been talking with God. (Exodus 34:29)*

One way of describing prayer is 'talking to God'. Few of
us can claim to have done so in the immanent way that
Moses did. One way of seeing this passage is that being
closely connected to God means that all is right with
us – and it shows. In what is essentially a reflection on
John 10:10, St Irenaeus said that 'the glory of God is the
human being fully alive'. There are many ways in which
we can shine as God intends.

Owning and using the goodness that is in each of
us is a significant way that we become fully alive and
appreciating other's giftedness also builds community.
Realising God's closeness in prayer is a primary way to
be whole. As contemplatives like Richard Rohr (*www.cac.
org*) teach us, it is about seeing our continuous connection
with God and others. This wondrous river of Love holds
us, supports us and feeds us if we have the eyes to see.
My glimpses leave me thirsting for more...

3 *February*

The Lord has done great things for us. (Psalm 126:3)

Things can change in our lives without notice. Thus
fostering a sense of gratitude for things as they are now
is very important. Closely allied to gratitude is a sense
of 'enough' – putting down what seems like a dominant
societal ethic of a relentless search for 'more'. We can be

grateful and feel like we have or are enough if we also have a sense of how God has gifted me – in terms of talents, relationships and material goods.

Our year can begin with an attitude of 'here we go again'. Or we can cultivate a sense of gratitude and of having and being enough based in our giftedness through God. Then we are much more likely to feel happy and whole, build our communities... and do great things.

4 *February*

But I say to you, Love your enemies and pray for
those who persecute you, so that you may be children
of your Father in heaven. (Matthew 5:44-45)

Does it get any harder or more real than this? This passage goes against what is called 'human nature' – we want to strike back against those who have hurt us or 'our own'. What this passage does is remind us about our *real* nature. We are made from and for love – since we are all children of God who is love. However, saying it and doing it are separate matters!

We need to try to act in a way that *includes* everyone, that ignores human-made divisions and treats everyone as *one*. When we pray for those who *only* see division, our prayer comes from a place of love: what we say and what we do and what we pray are as one.

5 February

On the day I called, you answered me,
you increased my strength of soul. (Psalm 138:3)

This cry of the heart aptly describes the human condition – being in need. The strength we ask for is not physical but strength to 'deal' with what life throws at us – strength of soul. If you ask and keep asking and are never answered, you're likely to give up. Yet, the fact that you're reading this means that you have felt 'answered' or have not lost hope. My prayer is that you continue to feel strengthened by our God.

6 February

Wait for the Lord;
be strong, and let your heart take courage.
(Psalm 27:14)

The Psalms echo down the millennia because they name the human condition and point the way. Any number of matters can try our patience or our hope. We can feel assaulted from without. Maybe we could look within, letting our 'heart take courage'. We can try to remember all that God has done for us in the past. We could trust in our God-given gifts and talents. Do we 'wait for the Lord' or do we wait for the fog of our own emotions to lift long enough for us to realise that the Lord never went away?

7 February

Thus says the Lord: I will put my law within them,
and I will write it on their hearts; and I will be their
God, and they shall be my people. (Jeremiah 31:33)

This passage has links to the ethics of natural law: people are born with a sense of right and wrong. For the vast majority of people, this passage holds true. And yet, we can know the good and choose otherwise – for a variety of reasons. These compulsions, addictions or whatever they are, blind us to the good – and prevent us from listening to our hearts.

And so we return to the importance of prayer and reflection. They are the opportunities to *stop*, listen to our heart, take stock of where we are headed. We can think we are carried along by the tide of life, neglecting to see the choices we have made – and the consequences of those choices. The cure to our problem is there – but it may not be easy.

8 February

Baby with her parents
Eyes wide
Soaking it all in
Happy
Smiling at everyone
Secure in love
From her parents
Which gives her the freedom
To grow
And absorb all around
With eyes of wonder
Reminding us to do likewise
And savour God's handiwork

9 February

*In this you rejoice, even if now for a little while
you have had to suffer various trials, so that the
genuineness of your faith– being more precious than
gold that, though perishable, is tested by fire – may be
found to result in praise and glory and honour when
Jesus Christ is revealed. (1 Peter 1:6-7)*

When we get past the freshness of the new year, there
may be incidents that brings us 'back to earth'. We are
then forced back to our 'why'. Why do I do the work
that I do? Every other reason melts away in time (like
impurities in a furnace?) until we are left with our faith.
Yet our faith is not just individual. We are saved in and

by community. Our community sustains us in good and bad times – just as we go out in faith and service to others.

10 *February*

But we have this treasure in clay jars, so that
it may be made clear that this extraordinary
power belongs to God and does not come from us.
(2 Corinthians 4:7)

It's so easy for us to be carried away by our egos! We often 'believe our own press' and can scheme for our own advancement. Whether our schemes are successful or not, we can be left feeling empty. Our faults and failings will bring us down to earth. Yes, we each have our gifts and it is right to treasure and develop them – but *praise* must go to the giver – God.

In community, my faults are compensated by another's strengths and vice versa. The beauty of the body of Christ!

11 February

Trust in the Lord with all your heart,
and do not rely on your own insight. (Proverbs 3:5)

If I trust in the Lord with all my heart, then I live believing in my unique giftedness, as well as the goodness and giftedness of those around me. Whether they believe in themselves is another matter! Life raises difficulties of all sorts. The extent to which we can trust in the Lord rather than rely on our own insight will determine how much those difficulties 'knock us off course'.

The Gospel message is not complicated – but our world has so many competing messages. For better or worse, the 'quick fix' is prized. One thing I have learned is that the Gospel message requires much practice to live well. Another thing I have learned is that, if I rely on my own insight, 'there lies madness'.

12 February

'Who are you, God, and who am I?' (St Francis)

This prayer was frequently on the lips of St Francis. As much as anyone, Francis understood the unity, the connection of all creation. We are so used to thinking in binary or dualistic terms: off/on, good/bad, us/them. Such thinking can blind us to our connection with others – in God. This connection commences at our beginning – when we are *each* loved into life. For most of us, the love of family and friends guides us on our journey towards our wholeness. Since we believe that

God is love (1 John 4:8), God is constantly present with us, in us and our family and friends.

One answer to 'who are you, God?' is the author of life, constantly present – in love. One answer to 'who am I?' is a creature lovingly created who finds their wholeness in love, like the Trinitarian God in whose image we were made.

13 February

Our soul waits for the Lord;
he is our help and shield. (Psalm 33:20)

When the going is tough, it is easy to feel isolated. The use of the plural pronoun binds us together. The reality is that we each 'come undone' and are in need of assistance. Rather than being unusual, this is to be embraced. Yet, it is not 'on tap'. We must be patient and wait, possibly to hear the 'still, small voice' (1 Kings 19:12). This statement of faith and hope rings true across the millennia.

The beauty of faith and patience is that they help us to step back from the demands and worries of the world. They help to give us a fresh perspective. Rather than be tossed one way and another by life's demands and worries, faith and patience give us the space to be and to grow into everything God gifted us. No small gift.

14 *February*

The Lord said, so shall my word be that goes out from my mouth;
it shall not return to me empty,
but it shall accomplish that which I purpose,
and succeed in the thing for which I sent it.
(Isaiah 55:11)

'You have my word' is an expression indicating the truth or fullness of our intention. I say I will and I do so. Much more than a human intention, God's word is so rich and multi-faceted. God's word guides us, corrects us, inspires us, warns us. God's word sets out a long-term plan for humanity, fully aware of our faults and failings but equally aware of our individual goodness and giftedness.

I glimpse and perhaps grasp that God's word is for *me*. It is not set in the past but, if I am open, can speak to the heart of each person. God's word speaks to my failings and my yearnings. This plan directs me home, into the arms of the God who loved me into life.

15 February

Frangipani
Dormant
For so long
Tended with love
If not always
With knowledge
Eagerly expected
As the signs increased
And grew more hopeful.
It's only a flower
Yet it's a symbol
Of connection
With my past;
Also of persistence;
But most powerfully
It is a symbol
Of God's grace
Of the delicate beauty
All around us
So long as
We have the eyes
To see

16 February

Great are the works of the Lord,
studied by all who delight in them. (Psalm 111:2)

To be able to say and assent to the first phrase of this passage requires faith. What follows is appreciation and gratitude for those around me and all created things, including myself. This is the beginning of sanity and wisdom. The second phrase implies that it is wise to be students of nature, of others and ourselves. Thus, as much as we can, it is in our best interests to appreciate and savour the gifts of nature, as well as exhibiting understanding and compassion towards others and ourselves.

Time and focus are required for each of us to be grateful and appreciate everything around us. When we take time to focus on what matters, we will know ourselves better and be better placed to exhibit understanding and compassion to others... and ourselves.

17 February

In every nation anyone who fears God and does what
is right is acceptable to him. (Acts 10:35)

This reading is set when the disciples were discerning who could be part of the Church. Was it to just be Jews, as most of them were? Their answer, as we know, was a much broader, more inclusive Church. 'Does what is right' is a translation of a word meaning 'justice and right relationships' i.e. what must be done to bring

God's reign. Between that and someone who reveres God – you can't ask much more from a person.

In our flawed humanity, we can fall short of our ideals. It is wise to be gentle with ourselves (and those around us) when we inevitably fall short. By displaying compassion, we act in the image of God.

18 February

Learn to do good;
seek justice,
*   rescue the oppressed,*
*   defend the orphan,*
*   plead for the widow. (Isaiah 1:17)*

We can focus on 'being good'. Isaiah reminds us of the importance of actions – *doing* good. The formula outlined in this passage is repeated in the Hebrew scriptures – look after those on the margins of society. Look after those crushed by 'the system' (the oppressed) and those who have no connection to society and thus no 'safety net' (the orphan and the widow).

Such actions focus not on GDP nor KPIs but focus on 'the other' – not me, but we. When my focus is other-directed, I become more whole as do those in need and thus our society. This is the path to wholeness and holiness.

19 *February*

Philip asked, 'Do you understand what you are reading?' The Ethiopian replied, 'How can I, unless someone guides me?' (Acts 8:30-31)

Whether it is a book of scripture or the book of my life, I need a reliable guide. That could be someone who has demonstrated knowledge and wisdom on a topic or someone who has lived life and reflected upon it. There is no shortage of information today but does it guide and nurture me?

A guide rounds out the details and cares about whether I truly understand. Jesus has 'the words of eternal life' (John 6:68). We must nurture ourselves by listening to Jesus – through scripture, prayer and the Eucharist.

20 *February*

For with you is the fountain of life. (Psalm 36:9)

It is easy to feel 'dried out' by life. It might be my own worries and concerns OR it could be observing the difficulties of others, near or far. Yet, we are nourished and replenished by God. How?

We are nourished by our relationships with others (since God is love – 1 John 4:8) and God through prayer. I am nourished by my community (when two or three are gathered in my name I am with you – Matthew 18:20). We are also nourished by God's word in the scriptures as well as the Eucharist. We need to remember to use all of these as frequently and as consciously as we can.

21 February

Repent and believe in the gospel. (Mark 1:15)

Who wants to admit that they are wrong? That it is rare is why someone is called a 'big person' if they do admit their mistakes. We need to engage in personal reflection so that we can be the best version of ourselves. To repent means to admit to yourself your limitations, your selfishness. To repent is to admit that you have missed opportunities to treat others with love and/or respect.

We need to abandon a definition of 'to believe' being intellectual assent in favour of 'to set your heart' upon something. If I set my heart upon the gospel, I set my heart upon being a disciple of Jesus. The Gospel calls me to reflect daily that I am living up to such a lofty goal. I set my heart upon being a conduit for love, compassion and respect – and so bringing closer the full life to which we are all called.

22 February

Have you ever seen waves?
Really *seen* them?
On a bright clear morning
Walking our dogs with my soul mate
I was struck
By their *layers*

We know that waves come into the shore.
Seen that.
Get that.
But on this peaceful day
There were so many
Waves
Of different types and sizes.
Waves within waves within waves.

The prevailing swell
Would gather all this up
Rippling the surface
Of this panoply of waves
Like a blanket flows
When shaken to make a bed.

A physicist's delight:
The waves would
Bounce and refract
Around obstructions.
Moving in four different directions

Including bouncing back out
From the shore.

There are so many layers
To God's grandeur.
I was graced
To glimpse another
On this bright morning.

23 February

*Do you not know that you are God's temple and that
God's Spirit dwells in you? (1 Corinthians 3:16)*

Seeing myself as deserving of respect is crucial if I am
to lead a full life. Self-respect tells me I am 'enough'
as I am and shapes my relationships in a positive way.
Such personal reflection is always timely. Perhaps I
cannot forgive myself for some action or omission? Yet,
God *already* has. Our ability to forgive ourselves is also
likely to increase our compassion.

24 February

Jesus said, 'So therefore, none of you can become my disciple if you do not give up all your possessions'.
(Luke 14:33)

Trying to be a disciple of Jesus in a developed country in the 21st century means that this passage is very challenging. There are some who are able to live this command to its fullest – but they are exceptional. There are a couple of points relevant for us.

There is the way that possessions can *have* us, holding us back from being all that we can be and affecting our relationships. There is also the way that our consumption of resources affects others by depriving them of their due, along with the impact of that resource use on God's creation (and thus eventually back on us). Part of the genius of Christianity is that we are saved in and by community. We do well to each examine our possessions to ensure that they are the best for me... and us.

25 February

Jesus answered him, 'Those who love me will keep my word, and my Father will love them, and we will come to them and make our home with them'. (John 14:23)

As Christians, we believe that the Father, Son and Spirit exist in a mutual indwelling of love. All of creation is caught up in this giving and receiving of love. Humanity has free will and so can choose to be faithful (or not) to

God's word that draws us towards love, compassion and respect. If we live in a loving way, we are our best selves and live in right relationships with others. Thus we are drawn into God's very self – this is life to the full.

26 February

Happy are those who find fault with themselves
instead of finding fault with others. (Muhammad)

Over the last twenty years or so, there has been a great deal of ignorance and misinformation about Islam. This saying (*hadith*) from the prophet Muhammad, peace be upon him, reminds us how closely aligned our religions are (see Matthew 7:3-5; Luke 6:41-42). There have been many throughout history who have used religion to justify the evil in their hearts. We should not be surprised that it is happening today. What of the decades of sectarian violence in Northern Ireland 'done in God's name'?

It is wise to struggle with myself to be the best person I can be (the true meaning of 'jihad') rather than pointing the finger at anyone else.

27 February

I do not cease to give thanks for you as I remember you in my prayers. (Ephesians 1:16)

An incorrect idea about prayer can become prevalent – that prayer is just between the individual and God. This enhances the stereotype of God as 'indulgent parent' handing out 'goodies' if we 'ask nicely'. This passage is very much about community – the body of Christ. This passage is about appreciating the goodness in others. Thus prayer is about relationships – with God and others. It has long been a tradition in the Church to pray for others. They might be a departed loved one, someone who is in need of love and mercy, someone for whom we wish to give thanks or maybe someone with whom we wish to have a better relationship. I'm sure we each have stories of those prayers being answered. Encouraging such prayerful habits provides the constant reminder that it is about we – not just me.

28 February

Jesus said, 'This is my commandment, that you love one another as I have loved you'. (John 15:12)

Our culture has skewed the meaning of the word 'love' – towards something that is sweet and light and fluffy. The Greek used here is better translated as 'self-sacrificing love'. To love as Jesus did means to love fully, completely, until the end. We might be able to accomplish that for one or two people – wife, husband, partner, children –

but Jesus is asking the disciples to love each other in that way. This sets the bar high! But as much as we can do so, we strengthen our relationships immeasurably. We build community.

As much as each of us can love as Jesus did we will be being true to ourselves and our communities – living in the image of the God of love in whom we were created.

29 February

For everything there is a season, and a time for every matter under heaven. (Ecclesiastes 3:1)

In this case, it is the once-every-four-years leap day. While this date is special, particularly for those born on this day, it should be a case of 'business as usual' when it comes to my behaviour. In that sense, every day is an opportunity to add something special into another person's day. It could be the kind word, the thoughtful gesture, being enthusiastic. The gifts God gave me should be used every day to build community.

MARCH

1 March

Horizontal drapes
Of delicate clouds
In silvery white
Through to grey
Sky awash with blues
Through to oranges and apricots.
Miraculous, shimmering tableau
And salve
Largely ignored
By those travelling home
From their work.
And so the veil is drawn
On another day.

2 March

But as for that in the good soil, these are the ones who, when they hear the word, hold it fast in an honest and good heart, and bear fruit with patient endurance. (Luke 8:15)

Life can be difficult at times – which is why we need to hold fast to God's word, to get us through those times. This passage speaks of really internalising God's word – but not just in the heart, but 'an honest and good heart'. The implication being that honesty and goodness are synonymous with God.

We live in a time focused on immediate results. Thus it is interesting to note the countercultural tone of this passage that God's word 'bears fruit with patient endurance'. There is a sense of this being in *kairos*, in God's time.

3 March

Jesus said, 'Whoever serves me must follow me'.
(John 12:26)

There is a difference between *saying* that you're a disciple of Jesus and *being* a disciple of Jesus. Rather than just being full of high-sounding words, the true disciple lives their faith. They follow Jesus in their actions *and* their words. Following Jesus means following God's word of compassion and inclusion for those on the outer. Including those on the outer *isn't* 'doing them a favour'. Rather it is living our faith in the body of Christ – that *everyone* has something to offer and we are all the poorer without it. Following Jesus also means speaking the truth to power – an uncomfortable and potentially dangerous place to be.

4 March

John the Baptist proclaimed, 'Repent, for the kingdom of heaven has come near'. (Matthew 3:2)

The reality is that we never 'arrive'. We are always in need of personal renewal – repentance of our shortcomings. A place and time when 'all is well' can seem very remote. Here we are assured that 'the kingdom of heaven has come near'. But how do we 'get there'? The kingdom of heaven is marked by justice and right relationships. We are reminded that it is about people – who are made in the image of God. Are my relationships marked by honesty, fairness, integrity? Do I treat others justly?

5 March

I too decided, after investigating everything carefully from the very first, to write an orderly account for you, most excellent Theophilus, so that you may know the truth concerning the things about which you have been instructed. (Luke 1:3-4)

It is so easy to get confused and not fully understand. Sometimes I can need encouragement to admit that I 'don't get it'. Thus the Gospel of Luke was intended for those who'd already heard about Jesus but needed some kind of confirmation. The original disciples of Jesus were beginning to die and some may have asked 'what now'. For 21st century readers of the Gospel, doubts can also be present. The evangelist says to us – there is truth and certainty in what you have been taught. Some may think that if you are to believe you cannot have doubts. This passage tells us that doubt is one part of the faith journey.

6 *March*

Why do you see the speck in your neighbour's eye, but do not notice the log in your own eye? (Matthew 7:3)

It seems to be part of human nature to be able to see others' faults but not our own. I guess it is a function of the way we observe the world – we look out, not in. Yet, the person of integrity *must* look inwards so that they practise what they preach. Nothing is more hollow than to say one thing and do another. Importantly, I need to ensure that I have my act together before I start correcting others. Criticising others is a good way to get people offside. Working towards self-improvement displays a humble realism that builds community.

7 March

*When evening came, his disciples went down to the
lake, got into a boat, and started across the lake to
Capernaum. It was now dark, and Jesus had not yet
come to them. The lake became rough because a strong
wind was blowing. When they had rowed about three
or four miles, they saw Jesus walking on the lake and
coming near the boat, and they were terrified. But
he said to them, 'It is I; do not be afraid'. Then they
wanted to take him into the boat, and immediately
the boat reached the land towards which they were
going. (John 6:16-21)*

There are so many factors at work in this passage. The
disciples are committed, rowing a boat at night. Then
difficulties arise, normal help is a long way away and
they cannot see Jesus in their panic. Despite our fears
and failure to see Jesus is present with us – through all
our difficulties. Once we realise that, like the disciples,
we find our difficulties will evaporate and we will reach
our 'destination'. A prayerful, contemplative approach
will help to keep us stable, whole and holy.

8 March

Your brilliance
And majesty
Cut through
My early morning
Torpor

And awaken
My soul
My whole being
To hope
To joy

Just another sunrise?
Blessed to sense grace

9 *March*

*Jesus said, 'Again, truly I tell you, if two of you agree
on earth about anything you ask, it will be done for
you by my Father in heaven. For where two or three
are gathered in my name, I am there among them'.
(Matthew 18:19-20)*

The first point from this passage is: don't go it alone.
Wholeness and holiness lie in community. The wholeness
connects us to others but also we are connected to our
Trinitarian God – Father, Son and Spirit. It is because
we are connected in this way, and not going it alone
potentially led by our selfish delusions, that God is
present with us. And when God is with us, all things are
possible!

10 *March*

I sink in deep mire,
  where there is no foothold;
I have come into deep waters,
  and the flood sweeps over me. (Psalm 69:2)

This passage speaks of the worst kind of difficulty. This is way more than 'having a bad day'. If I am at this point, I am under no illusions I need help. Disaster is imminent. I know I cannot do it on my own. What do I do? I throw myself on God's mercy. Had I resisted doing so beforehand? Does it take disaster for me to call on God? Events can shape our lives. This can also be a moment of conversion. Will I finally and permanently turn to God?

11 *March*

To love souls for God, to love beings because they are
in the image of God, to love God in all created beings.
(Helene de Chappotin)

You may have heard the expression about 'being God's heart and hands'. By being compassionate towards others, we change others, the world and ourselves. Why do so? We are each a unique, unrepeatable image of God, imbued with dignity and worthy of respect. Loving in this way helps us to more fully grasp the awe-inspiring scale of God's project in humanity. Loving in this way draws us closer to the light – in others and ourselves. But Helene pushes it even further by including all beings so that our love is for all of God's creation. And there is so much to love! The created beings that do not draw us are an opportunity for our conversion to a more spacious idea of God's grandeur.

12 March

I believe, help my unbelief. (Mark 9:24)

Never a truer word spoken. I believe – while everything is going well and there are no obstacles. I believe – until I hit the wall. 'The wall' might be difficulties I strike that mean I forget I can't do it all. 'The wall' might be the opinions of others that I feel are deriding me. 'The wall' might be a situation I haven't struck before – and self-doubt creeps in. Another way to describe 'the wall' is my humanity, my failings. One solution is to not expect myself to do, know or be it all. Rather, be at home in my failings – and open to the ways I can be helped by other members of the body of Christ.

13 March

Then I acknowledged my sin to you,
and I did not hide my iniquity;
I said, 'I will confess my transgressions to the Lord',
and you forgave the guilt of my sin. (Psalm 32:5)

One way of looking at this passage is that God *already* knows and if I acknowledge my sins – it is primarily for *me*. Being in denial about my mistakes doesn't help me correct them or move on from them. Acknowledging my mistakes is likely to increase my compassion for others and make me less judgmental of the mistakes of others. If I acknowledge my mistakes, they have much less power over me. I do not have them weighing on my conscience and I am able to move on.

14 March

'If today you hear his voice, harden not your hearts.'
(Hebrews 3:10)

If I am a person of faith, why would I harden my heart to God's voice? An answer is because of its demands on me. God's voice might remind me to go out of my way to care for those in need who are another of God's creation. God's voice might remind me to turn aside from my selfish ways that has me using more than my share of the Earth's resources. God's voice might remind me to treat everyone in my life with dignity and respect since they are each made in the image of God. God's voice might remind me it is only right that those whom I say I love be shown love by me rather than taken for granted.

15 March

We are each
A composite
Of so many
Factors
Influences

Parents
Siblings
Home life
Deaths
Incidents
Friends
Education

But it comes down to choices.
How will I live?
Follow the Gospel.
Love:
Following my heart.
Worry about the plank
In my own eye
Rather than the speck
In someone else's.
Trust
Communication
Compassion
Integrity

16 March

We entreat you on behalf of Christ, be reconciled to
God. (2 Corinthians 5:20)

'May the body of Christ bring us to eternal life.' These words from the Eucharist remind us that we are saved in community, we are saved for community. We each have gifts and talents lovingly placed in us by God. Those gifts reach their fullness when we each use them to build community. We are reconciled to God when we accept who we truly are, what our gifts are, where those gifts come from and work with others to build community. This is the work of wholeness and holiness. So working on what makes *me* whole, helps to make my community more whole. The more gifts that are being used the more the body of Christ is being built up. This path of right relationships brings God's reign closer.

17 March   *St Patrick*

Then Jesus said to Simon, 'Do not be afraid; from
now on you will be catching people'. When they had
brought their boats to shore, they left everything and
followed him. (Luke 5:10-11)

While he was born into the Church with his father and grandfather being members of clergy, Patrick's impetus for faith was seeing God's hand at work in his life, literally saving him from death. After being taken to Ireland from England as a slave, he eventually escaped and subsequently studied for the priesthood.

He returned to Ireland as a priest and used his talents as teacher, orator with a hint of politician to win over the people of Ireland to Christ. Ireland has long been known as a bastion of Christianity and, as that information spread, so the seminal role of Patrick in the faith of the Irish has also spread. He taught that each day's rising is God's gift and his contemplative vision of Christ in his 'Breastplate' rings true through the centuries: 'Christ with me, Christ before me, Christ behind me, Christ in me'.

18 March

Even now, says the Lord,
return to me with your whole heart. (Joel 2:12)

Is it too late? The answer: it is never too late to return to God. We may judge ourselves or our behaviour as lacking somehow, even sinful. We might feel like a 'bad person'. This might occur because we have done something for which we can't forgive ourselves. But it is never too late. Staying stuck in guilt doesn't help. Seek forgiveness from those you've wronged. Be better. Move on. The important thing to note is that this can't be half-hearted. If I am half-hearted, I am torn. I don't know which way to go. Rather, I must be 'all in'. That way, I can focus and channel my energies into both being better *and* doing better especially for those around me.

19 *March*

During a beautiful celebration
At the cathedral
Where community was tangible
I realised that
I am held
In the arms
Of so many different people
That love and support me

Primarily, my darling wife,
Soul mate
My everything.
Also, my sons,
My mother,
My siblings,
And extended family
Including my in-laws

The list includes
My friends
Some of whom I'm lucky
To have had in my life
For many years
My colleagues
And former colleagues
Students
And former students

Around and under and over
All
Is our faith.
God IS our relationships
And so much more
As our finite words
Cannot describe the infinite.

This community of support is
The body of Christ
Which brings me
To eternal life.

Salvation is now

20 *March*

But Jesus called them to him and said, 'You know
that the rulers of the Gentiles lord it over them, and
their great ones are tyrants over them. It will not be
so among you; but whoever wishes to be great among
you must be your servant'. (Matthew 20:25-26)

The scriptures are very clear about what Christian leadership should look like. When it comes to reality, never doubt the power of the human ego! There are sufficient examples over the centuries to emphasise the point that is being made in this passage. Christian leadership is about building up the community – not a personality cult. Christian leadership gives credit and glory to God for all our gifts and talents – it is not about others bowing to a leader. Acting 'in the person of Christ' means acting with love, compassion, inclusion and forgiveness – not being put on a pedestal. The tough part is living it continuously and not allowing our egos to take over!

21 *March*

They cried out, 'Away with him! Away with him!
Crucify him!' Pilate asked them, 'Shall I crucify your
King?' The chief priests answered, 'We have no king
but the emperor'. (John 19:15)

John highlights where the Jews (who do not believe in Jesus) are not true to their own spiritual tradition. After the Babylonian exile, there would be no kings since God alone was king (theocracy). So John uses irony, showing the Jews happy to crucify the real, divine king in Jesus and willingly break their own faith by seeing the Roman emperor as the king. Is God the centre of my life? Am I distracted by money, possessions or power? And if so, what am I going to do about it?

22 March

Is not this the fast that I choose:
 to loose the bonds of injustice,
 to undo the thongs of the yoke,
to let the oppressed go free,
 and to break every yoke?
Is it not to share your bread with the hungry,
 and bring the homeless poor into your house;
when you see the naked, to cover them,
 and not to hide yourself from your own kin? *(Isaiah 58:6-7)*

What is the point of a spiritual practice? Surely, it is to be a better person. The problem is that through the centuries too many believers have been focused on following all of the rules, rather than on being a better person. And some spiritual leaders have also focused on the rules too much. 'The rules', such as fasting, are designed to turn my gaze outward so that I recognise the needs of others and my capacity to do something about their needs; to help where and when I can. I must remember that right relationships and justice bring God's reign closer.

23 March

I want to know Christ and the power of his
resurrection and the sharing of his sufferings by
becoming like him in his death. (Philippians 3:10)

Being a disciple of Jesus involves prayer, reflecting upon the scriptures and then acting upon them. It means loving as Jesus did – openly, with no reserve. It also means calling out those who treat people as commodities rather than the image of God that they are. And as we have seen over the centuries, acting in that way will get you pilloried and even killed. But by embracing this way of living, it leads to great life, a resurrection for a community. As St Oscar Romero said, just weeks prior to his killing: 'I have often been threatened with death. I must tell you, as a Christian, I do not believe in death without resurrection. If I am killed, I shall arise in the Salvadoran people. I say so without boasting, with the greatest humility.... A bishop will die, but God's church, which is the people, will never perish'. The question is: do I have the integrity and the courage?

24 March
For Oscar Romero

A life of integrity
And witness
Cut short by power,
Deaf and blind
To the inconvenient truth.

Your life
Freely given for faith
And love
Especially of the little ones
As you celebrated
God-with-us
With your very person.

Your deeds and words
Reverberate across the years
Touch my heart
And inspire me
To live
As a disciple

25 *March*   *Annunciation*

The Most Blessed Virgin lived her whole life by the spirit of faith, and it is this spirit that God wants you to have. This is why you would derive much benefit from asking her in prayer to lead you to Our Lord along this way. (John Baptist De La Salle)

Mary was the first disciple of Jesus and her life was marked by faith in God, beginning with her 'yes' to God at the Annunciation. Being a person of faith can be demanding, battling a variety of difficulties whether they are external or internal. But the point is that we do not battle them alone. We cannot do it all by ourselves but *with* God all things are possible. It does not magically fix things but you are no longer alone. There must have been horrible situations with which Mary had to deal but such a spirit of faith enabled her to continue. This spirit of faith, this active seeking of help and support, step by step, brings us closer to God.

26 *March*

And Mary said,
'My soul magnifies the Lord,
   and my spirit rejoices in God my Saviour'.
(Luke 1:46)

Mary was deliriously happy about being pregnant, sharing that time with her cousin Elizabeth and was glorifying God for all he had done for her. As humans of the 21st century, we must be careful not to read into the text (*eisegesis*) i.e. not put our stuff on the text, e.g. social stigma about being young and pregnant or questions about parentage.

We may find faith difficult – for a variety of reasons. Mary's example of faith in God is for today and all time. Mary expresses her joy and gratitude for all of God's gifts. Those times of elation are precious and to be savoured. One way that we might emulate Mary is by being open-hearted – open to life and all its experiences. How might I foster an attitude of being open-hearted?

27 March

Pilate asked him, 'So you are a king?' Jesus answered,
'You say that I am a king. For this I was born, and
for this I came into the world, to testify to the truth.
Everyone who belongs to the truth listens to my voice.'
Pilate asked him, 'What is truth?' (John 18:37-38)

The Gospel of John frequently uses misunderstanding as a narrative device. Here it highlights that Pilate does not see the world in the same way as Jesus. Rather than asking a seemingly philosophical question, readers of the Gospel know that Pilate is staring truth in the face. In fact, Pilate condemns himself because his response shows that he is not listening to Jesus and so does not belong to the truth. We might ponder: do I take time to listen to Jesus in prayer and scripture? Am I able to see the face of Jesus in others? Jesus is not king – he comes to wash our feet and he encourages us to do likewise. So our ideas about true leadership may need some adjustment...

28 March

Jesus said, 'Remove this cup from me; yet, not what I
want, but what you want'. (Mark 14:36)

When all is going well, it is easy to be good and/or to
have faith. The Gospel accounts of Jesus' passion give us
an insight into how difficult this time must have been.
Pushed to the limit, it's far easier to walk away: 'live
to fight another day'. Jesus turns that logic on its head
while still exhibiting his humanity. He doesn't want to
go to the cross but realises that his faith and integrity
require that of him.

These are vital life lessons. Will I stand up for what I
believe in? Will I walk away when the going gets tough?
Will I be a person of integrity? Will I have faith in God
in the tough times and believe in the reflection: 'it was
then that I carried you'? Our answers to such questions
can lead us to fullness of life.

29 March

And what should I say – "Father, save me from this
hour"? No, it is for this reason that I have come to
this hour. (John 12:27)

The Johannine Jesus knows his death is coming. He has
spoken the truth to power – the result is inevitable. We
have seen this pattern in recent times in such people as
Dietrich Bonhoeffer, Martin Luther King Jr and Oscar
Romero. In John's Gospel, there is constant reference
to 'the hour', beginning at the wedding feast at Cana

in Chapter 2. The hour is both when Jesus is crucified ('lifted up') and glorifies God. The Johannine Jesus, as he has throughout, has his eyes wide open about his journey: he does the work of the Father and is to glorify the Father.

In the realisation of what is coming for Jesus, there is a choice – stay the course or walk away. And so it is for all of us – am I a person of integrity? OR would I rather ignore my conscience and take the easy choice?

30 March

When Jesus saw his mother and the disciple whom he loved standing beside her, he said to his mother, 'Woman, here is your son'. Then he said to the disciple, 'Here is your mother'. And from that hour the disciple took her into his own home. (John 19:26-27)

This is a human moment. In the midst of his agony on the cross, Jesus sees his mother and knows she will suffer even more without someone to help her. The beloved disciple (John?) can fill the gap left by Jesus and care for Mary. This is likely a divine moment as well. At the foot of the cross the church is born – the community beginning with Mary and the beloved disciple. In what ways do I accept Jesus in 'my own home'? In what ways do I build community by building relationships? Do I see and call forth the good in others?

31 March

Then Jesus bowed his head and gave up his spirit.
(John 19:30)

Given all that has come before, this is the moment of
Jesus' death. Yet, another translation is that Jesus 'gave
down the spirit'. This translation means the completion
of everything of which Jesus has spoken – Jesus' death
brings the Holy Spirit. Despite Jesus' death, the Holy
Spirit is present to accompany the believer. It also fulfils
'the hour' – that Jesus' death on the cross brings about
the glory of God through the coming of the Holy Spirit.
In what ways am I aware of the Holy Spirit in my life?

April

85

1 April

*The fruit of the Spirit is love, joy, peace, patience,
kindness, generosity, faithfulness, gentleness, and self-
control. (Galatians 5:22-23)*

Each day we have a choice. Will we focus on the
momentary euphoria of the day OR are our lives set on
the path to joy? Joy comes from a life seeking justice
through right relationships lived in self-sacrificing love.
It is indeed a journey – sometimes two steps forward, one
step back OR maybe the other way around! This is the
truth of the way of the disciples of Jesus – the only true
way forward is through the cross. The difficulties and
the successes are shared as we live our lives in the image
of our God – in community.

Momentary euphoria is nice and has its place
but it can be a distraction from 'the main game' – living
a life for others that creates an inclusive community.
Throughout the coming twelve months may we each live
lives on the path to joy, since 'joy is the infallible sign of
the presence of God' (Teilhard de Chardin).

2 April

And now faith, hope, and love abide, these three; and
the greatest of these is love. (1 Corinthians 13:13)

Humans can relate to suffering. Humans endure a great deal - the loss of family or friends; being bullied or disrespected; abuse of whatever kind; the seemingly endless labyrinths of addiction or mental health issues. But how are we freed from this suffering?

God's answer, indeed the only answer that makes sense, is love. Love does not make problems magically disappear but is the most powerful force for transformation. Love builds community. Love shares the burden. Love cures hurts and helps make us whole. Love helps to shine a light in the darkness. As Martin Luther King Jr said: 'Hate cannot drive out hate. Only love can do that'.

May we also celebrate the ways that love binds us together, frees us from difficulties and transforms our lives – remembering that God is love.

3 April

Very truly, I tell you, unless a grain of wheat falls into the earth and dies, it remains just a single grain; but if it dies, it bears much fruit. (John 12:24)

As humans, we want a 'satisfying' end – whether that is the end of a story, the end of a phase of our lives or the end of a life. If the ending is untimely or there are 'loose ends', our brains will 'worry away' at such matters until a 'completion' can be found. The disciples of Jesus suffered a devastating loss at his death. It was only after the resurrection of Jesus when they turned his words over and over in their minds that they found an answer much broader than Jesus.

This type – the death that gives life – they finally saw in many places, including nature. With this faith, disciples of Jesus found the grace and strength to withstand persecutions and many other difficulties. With this faith, an individual life helps to build a community. This logic is still counterintuitive, as I suspect it always will be. We must each ponder its truth in the light of our lives. With God's grace the pattern will continue.

4 April

The leaders of the people kept looking for a way to kill
Jesus; but they did not find anything they could do,
for all the people were spellbound by what they heard.
    (Luke 19:47-48)

Whether it is the Gospels, the reflections of the mystics or our modern sage, Michael Leunig, they outline that human actions and reactions can be attributed to the choice between fear or love. Love is arresting and attractive because it is in sharp counterpoint to fear. There were many forces at work in first century Palestine but one way of reading this passage juxtaposes the fear of the 'leaders of the people' with the love of Jesus. Jesus' love seen in his preaching and ministry was attractive – thus 'the people were spellbound'.

    With this in mind, it is wise to reflect upon our actions and reactions to discern how many come from a place of love and how many come from a place of fear. Am I practising what I preach? And if I don't like what I see, how am I going to change? They are difficult but important questions for us to answer so that we can live life to the full.

5 April

Jesus is 'the stone that was rejected by you, the
builders; it has become the cornerstone'. (Acts 4:11)

Humans can overlook something that is in plain sight.
The Gospels tell us that Jesus' preaching and teaching
annoyed the Jewish authorities – so much so that they
were willing to kill him. There can be argument about
whether Jesus was killed for religious or political reasons
(or some combination) – but his rejection is clear.

This invites the question: why, over two millennia,
have millions found Jesus to be 'the cornerstone'? He
lived a life of integrity – he lived his faith in God through
care and compassion for those in need. Like the prophets
before him, he called those in power to account – is God
above all? Pivotally, Jesus showed us what God is like,
having an intimate love for each person. Jesus also calls
us to be our best selves by building community through
being in right relationship with all.

6 April

Jesus said, 'I am the good shepherd. The good
shepherd lays down his life for the sheep'. (John 10:11)

Jesus cares for us, his sheep. He does so in the ultimate
way by laying down his life. Communities need good
shepherds. Both past and present are littered with
examples of bad shepherds. Bad shepherds do not build
up the flock, individually nor collectively. Bad shepherds
do not draw out and give opportunities to develop each

person's gifts and abilities. Bad shepherds are focused on an agenda that makes *them* look good. There is little if any personal cost in such leadership. I pray that, like me, you have known good shepherds – and do all you can to follow their example.

7 April   Feast of John Baptist De La Salle

Let us remember that we are in the holy presence of God. (John Baptist De La Salle)

On this feast day of John Baptist De La Salle, the patron saint of Christian educators, there is so much you could say. I have chosen this because it is simple and powerful. We are constantly in God's presence where God is totally 'other' in a way that we can't wrap our heads around. And yet, God is also present, through the Incarnation, in each one of us. It is easy to forget one or both of these powerful truths – so we must be reminded so we do not forget. We do not 'put ourselves in God's presence' – we are already there. The extension of this is that if God is present in me and everyone else then I need to respect myself and my relationships should also be imbued with respect. Genius – inspired by the Holy Spirit.

8 April

Eyes closed
Man snuggled
Against woman
Against wall
Of the train carriage
Arm of one placed
Lovingly
Around the other

Long day
Hard work
A study in
Shared fatigue
At day's end

9 April

But many who are first will be last, and the last will be first. (Mark 10:31)

Many of us can cheer for the underdog whether it is in sport or other parts of life. When you're not personally involved, it is easier to be dispassionate. What if the 'great overturning' includes me? We each do well to consider the ways we are more fortunate than others both for the sake of gratitude but also we can be aware of how we can give to others – of our time, of our gifts, of our relative plenty. Such a community focus brings God's reign closer.

10 April

*If you then, who are evil, know how to give good gifts
to your children, how much more will the heavenly
Father give the Holy Spirit to those who ask him!
(Luke 11:13)*

The Holy Spirit guides us into the truth (John 16:13) about ourselves, about others, about life. Part of that truth is coming to understand more fully who I am and my giftedness. The Holy Spirit also sustains us through the difficult times that come. The Holy Spirit is an extraordinary gift – and all we have to do is ask! Such is the love from our God who loved each of us into being.

I come to realise that living life to the full is not a project I can achieve alone. It is through prayer and reflection that I grow in self-knowledge – and grow in my understanding of my limitations and thus my need of support – from God and those around me. The Holy Spirit will guide me to see the gifts God has placed in me and help me to use them to build community.

11 April

*Simeon blessed them and said to his mother Mary,
'This child is destined for the falling and the rising
of many in Israel, and to be a sign that will be
opposed so that the inner thoughts of many will be
revealed – and a sword will pierce your own soul too'.
(Luke 2:34-35)*

As a young mother, it must have been very difficult for Mary – with her faith being tried on many occasions. There isn't even the chance to rejoice in her new baby without having to face a troubling future. The prospect of having my inner thoughts revealed is a very challenging notion. Yet our thoughts and words guide our actions. There will always be a gap between the words of the disciples of Jesus and their actions. Our task is to make that gap as small as possible. The gap may be due to power, prestige, insecurity. The smaller the gap between our words and our actions, the more likely we will have our soul pierced, like Mary; doing the thing that is right but difficult.

12 April

*I am utterly spent and crushed;
I groan because of the tumult of my heart.
(Psalm 38:8)*

In the midst of our difficulties, we need to vent and we need to feel supported. Friends and family can be vital at such times – and are part of the body of Christ. Being honest with God in prayer is important – remembering that God can catch whatever is thrown! Such honesty can help us truly surface our thoughts and feelings. This can provide a way forward and maybe even some healing. At such times, it is also important to remember the solace that can be provided by scripture and the sacraments.

13 April

Again Jesus spoke to them, saying, 'I am the light of the world. Whoever follows me will never walk in darkness but will have the light of life'. (John 8:12)

Again, Jesus' divinity is explicit in this 'I am' saying but being 'light of the world' is the focus. We are drawn to the light – to its comfort and consolation. It is easy to feel 'in the dark'. No matter the pain, loneliness, addiction, heartbreak or whatever – Jesus' way of living and loving directs us. By following Jesus, we are directed towards showing love and compassion for all around us, especially those on the margins. We are also directed towards prayer and scripture. This all leads us on the path to the light – of wholeness and holiness.

14 April

Jesus said, 'Anyone who comes to me I will never drive away'. (John 6:37)

This passage needs to be read with the backdrop of the separation between Jews and Christians in the late Ist century CE that helps to date John's Gospel. Thus the reader/believer will not be driven away because of what they believe, what is central or deeply personal. The separation between Jews and Christians would have been intensely painful, personal. As a 21st century reader, there are times when we can feel that we do not belong, we do not fit in, sometimes because of our faith. The believer will always have a home with Jesus. Why? The Christian community. Do you have a Christian community where you feel at home? Do you help your Christian community be a place of welcome?

15 April

Walk out my door
Into the early morning dark
And as my eyes adjust
I look up
Into the inky sky
And am dazzled
By the stars.
They make me
Catch my breath
And utter 'thanks'

For this gift.
Plain
Ordinary
Wondrous

16 April

Jesus taught them as one having authority, and not as their scribes. (Matthew 7:29)

We live in a world with so much 'chatter'. Many want to stake a claim on our time or allegiance but we recognise that so much of it is empty. We know we cannot rely on ourselves alone, so who will guide us? Essentially, we are looking for someone of integrity who practises what they preach. We crave this wholeness but we know we fall short and need to be reminded: 'this is what integrity looks like'. It is attractive but costly as more recent examples like Dietrich Bonhoeffer, Oscar Romero, Mother Teresa and Malala Yousafzai have shown us.

17 April

*A woman named Martha welcomed Jesus into her
home. She had a sister named Mary, who sat at the
Lord's feet and listened to what he was saying. But
Martha was distracted by her many tasks; so she
came to him and asked, 'Lord, do you not care that
my sister has left me to do all the work by myself?
Tell her then to help me'. But the Lord answered her,
'Martha, Martha, you are worried and distracted by
many things; there is need of only one thing. Mary has
chosen the better part, which will not be taken away
from her'. (Luke 10:38-42)*

We know this story and it is the tension, the seeming
unfairness that provides the lesson to us. We live in a
world of busyness so Martha's diligence and attention to
detail seems praiseworthy. What Jesus does is lift the veil
on Martha's behaviour – that there is a driven, obsessive
edge to it. A lesson is that in order for work to have
meaning it must be fed by reflection and contemplation.
Another twist in this story is that we all have Martha
and Mary within us and we need to hold our action and
contemplation in a creative tension where one feeds the
other.

18 April

*It is not fitting, when one is in God's service, to have a
gloomy face or a chilling look. (St Francis of Assisi)*

Another way of looking at this is in terms of the 'good

news'. If we are living 'good news' then that rules out 'a gloomy face or a chilling look'. We must *be* good news. We are all different and 'upbeat' looks different for different people. It does *not* mean you can never be sad. Trying times come to us all but faith in the good news helps us to transcend those trying times. Also, people 'read' us. 'You say you believe in the good news? How good is it really?' May we each be up to the challenge of living the good news.

19 April

It is easier for a camel to go through the eye of a needle than for someone who is rich to enter the kingdom of God. (Mark 10:25)

While this analogy may not be as stark for 21ˢᵗ century readers, we know that large animals do not fit through the eye of a needle. The kingdom of God is about a focus on *people in community*. Why might it be so difficult for a rich person to enter the kingdom of God? Might it be that their focus is not on people, but on things? Might it be that their focus is too narrow, too selfish? Before I start thinking 'this passage is not about me. I'm not rich', it would be good to consider the focus of my life – self or others?

20 *April*

If I say, 'I will not mention him,
or speak any more in his name',
then within me there is something like a burning fire
shut up in my bones;
I am weary with holding it in,
and I cannot. (Jeremiah 20:7)

You may or may not relate to this passage. You may be on a different path of the faith journey. The more important point from this passage is: am I true to myself and my faith? We must each be true to ourselves. We know of the importance of our physical health, primarily through diet and exercise. There is a growing appreciation of mental health. Spiritual health is closely allied to mental health. Ensuring I take time for me, do things that recharge my batteries and build my relationships contribute to my spiritual health as much as my mental health. We may not share Jeremiah's take on faith but time for prayer and reflection will help stoke the flame of faith within.

21 *April*

Whoever is not against us is for us. (Mark 9:40)

It is easy to fall into the trap of seeing the world – and especially the people in it – as 'good' or 'bad'. Our society can abound with such 'binary' thinking. When we reflect upon matters, we may realise that those 'against us' are quite small in number, however powerful they

may seem at any given moment. Thus the vast majority
are 'for us' – or at least not putting obstacles in our way.

22 April

Choose life so that you and your descendants may
live, loving the Lord your God, obeying him, and
holding fast to him (Deuteronomy 30:19-20)

Choose life? Who would knowingly choose death?
Instead, it may be choosing an existence – which could be
bland, or worse, in shadow. As I look around the world,
there are people who lead an existence in the shadows.
Did they choose? Maybe not consciously. Surely we love
God by obeying and holding fast to him. But what does
this look like? It means becoming aware of the teachings
in scripture and following them, constantly – not just
when I feel like it. 'Love your neighbor as yourself' is
a double-edged sword, building respect of community
and self. I love God through a prayerful relationship.
Living this way brings life. Anything else is just existing.

23 April

What is the kingdom like?
A place where our words
Fall short
Where goodness
Kindness and
Decency are
The norm
Are not
Remarkable
A community
Where needs are
Cared for
Where everyone is
Valued

For now
Glimpses
Must suffice

The grace of a young woman
Helping with great care and little fuss
An older blind woman
Get off a train

The simple joy
Of young children
As they embrace
Each moment
Of living

The happiness and
Acceptance
Radiated
By the man
On his daily walk

We're not there
Yet
But such
Graced glimpses
Remind us of
Where we're headed
With God's guidance

24 April

'Which of these three, do you think, was a neighbour
to the man who fell into the hands of the robbers?' He
said, 'The one who showed him mercy'. Jesus said to
him, 'Go and do likewise'. (Luke 10:36-37)

In a developed country as an urban dweller, our idea of
neighbour can become skewed. Now it means 'someone
who lives near me' but not necessarily 'another member
of our community'. Such bonds have been loosened in
a world that has become increasingly individualistic. In
the time of Jesus, a neighbour is 'someone like you who
has claims upon your time and energy'. What it is wise to
remember is that since we believe that God is our father
then we are *all* sisters and brothers – we are all connected.
Indeed what unites us is much greater than what divides
us. So, despite our failings (or maybe because of them?)
we are guided to show mercy to everyone. How's that for
a challenge!

25 April

Let people think what they wish of you, and do not
be troubled, provided you are doing what you ought.
(John Baptist De La Salle)

We humans can frequently be very concerned with what
others think. Living in community, this can be a helpful
trait, so as not to cause offence or upset. However, to
ensure a community is thriving, there must also be
an encouragement of diversity. So long as you are not

directly hurting another, you may say and do as you please. This is especially the case if you are following your heart and/or your faith. Such expressions can enrich the community. 'Doing as you ought' means imitating Jesus by caring for those in need, treating others with love and compassion, engaging in prayer and using my gifts and talents to build community. And don't worry about the haters!

26 April

Thomas answered Jesus, 'My Lord and my God!'
(John 20:28)

'Don't be a doubting Thomas.' Thomas has copped a lot over the centuries. Not present at Jesus' first appearance among the Twelve, his pragmatic stance would be applauded these days! While Thomas' doubting is remembered, what isn't remembered is his response to Jesus. In terms of believing in this gospel, Thomas passes with flying colours. He acknowledges Jesus' divinity and he falls to the ground in worship. Rather than focus on the fact that Thomas 'got it wrong' to start with, it might be more important to focus on the fact that he got it right in the end. And maybe we can be as kind to others and ourselves.

27 April

Then they told what had happened on the road, and
how Jesus had been made known to them in the
breaking of the bread. (Luke 24:35)

What is the resurrection? The simple answer is that it defies easy categories. Inasmuch as the resurrection is for us, it is an expression of infinite love and so there will be many 'answers'. One answer is that the disciples on the road to Emmaus discerned the presence of Jesus in the Eucharist. It was then that 'their eyes were opened'. And so it is for us – when the believing community gathers for the Eucharist, Jesus is present. Will we have the eyes to see Jesus? In the congregation? In the celebrant? In the scriptures? In the bread and wine?

28 April

But these are written so that you may come to
believe that Jesus is the Messiah, the Son of God, and
that through believing you may have life in his name.
(John 20:31)

The (first) conclusion of John's Gospel does not pretend to be a history – it is a faith document. It is written 'that you may come to believe'. The verb 'believe' is used 114 times in John's Gospel – never the noun faith. One point we take from that is our faith must be *lived*, acted upon. It is not just a set of creedal statements. Another point is that Jesus is the fulfillment of the Hebrews Scriptures, the Messiah, and that he is divine. Crucially,

this believing in Jesus is intended to give each of us life –
now. Does the Gospel live up to this lofty promise? That
is for you to decide.

29 April

God saw everything that he had made, and indeed, it
was very good. (Genesis 1:31)

St Francis pointed the way for humanity to glimpse
God's good work in all of creation. In what ways is it
good? Not only that it is perfectly made, nor that it has
a purpose (whether humans can grasp that or not), nor
that it can be utilised by humanity – though these are
all true. The heart of the goodness are the multiple and
subtle connections, the way it all *works*. Humans are
part of this extraordinary tableau whether we wish to
acknowledge it or not. Can I open my mind to glimpse
what God has put in train? Can I allow myself to be
buoyed by the beauty in God's creation, seeing God's
reflection?

30 *April*

I will give thanks to the Lord with my whole heart;
I will tell of all your wonderful deeds. (Psalm 9:1)

An attitude of gratitude is important as everything we have and all that we are is gift. It is not *ours* – it can be gone in a moment. Sometimes life can teach us that lesson, painfully. All the more reason to value our gifts – of relationships, of possessions, of life – in this time called 'the present'. These gifts are so basic, so vital, that the only appropriate response is *wholehearted* thanks. Acknowledging our gifts and the giver helps our focus to be correct – *not* on ourselves. Now more than ever, telling our story of gratitude is precious. That 'small stone in the pond' will create ripples, nudging the world towards wholeness and holiness.

MAY

1 May

*Jesus said to them, 'I am the bread of life. Whoever
comes to me will never be hungry, and whoever
believes in me will never be thirsty'. (John 6:35)*

John's Gospel doesn't have a last supper where the
Eucharist is modelled. Rather there is this extensive
reflection on the Eucharist – set in the synagogue at
Capernaum. The 'I am' sayings in this Gospel indicate
the divinity of Jesus and point to what God does for us.
If we follow the example of Jesus – his obedience to God,
his loving, compassionate relationships – we will be
whole. If we believe in Jesus we will not go through life
constantly searching, looking for the 'the next thing'.

We can ask: Who am I? What is my unique role
in life? How can I be happy? We must remember that
we are good *as we are*. Coming to Jesus, coming to God is
to believe in God-with-us – which is the same as being a
member of a community – building up others and being
built up by them in turn. Our needs are met… and we are
resting in God.

2 May

*Jesus is the image of the invisible God, the firstborn
of all creation; for in him all things in heaven and
on earth were created, things visible and invisible,
whether thrones or dominions or rulers or powers –
all things have been created through him and for him.
(Colossians 1:15-16)*

All our language about God will fall short. How can I describe the infinite with our finite language? Thus metaphor and analogy are used. The point of this passage is that God is in everything and brought everything to be. The fact that my theories or my knowledge may come up against a brick wall is *my* problem. Such an impasse can cause some to reject God. In fact what they are rejecting is a limited understanding of God – and that is good. Our understanding of God should be spacious (to quote Timothy Radcliffe OP). It also challenges us to see God's hand at work *everywhere*. This is indeed challenging – but worth the work!

3 *May*

Sing joyfully to the Lord. (Psalm 98:4)

To be able to sing to the Lord, I must first be aware of the good in my life both in me and around me. If I am to sing to the Lord then I believe in God and believe that it is right to be grateful to the giver of all the goodness in my life – God. Then there is the adverb 'joyfully'. We can engage in behaviours where we are 'doing the right thing' – some degree of obligation is involved. When all that we are and all that we have is gift, it is only fitting that our thanks for these gifts is without reserve. Everything may not go our way but let us each make the most of this gift called life.

4 May

Jesus said, 'I am the light of the world'. (John 9:5)

We need light to guide us. There will be times when all is going well and we can find our own way. But when things turn sour, as they do, who or what will guide us? When I feel selfish, who better to remind me of the wholeness and holiness of a life lived for others? When I feel aimless who better to remind me of the path? This is the same path that St Francis of Assisi glimpsed when he said: 'it is in giving that we receive'. When I am lost in the darkness of grief, who better to remind me that suffering and death do not have the last word? May you glimpse that light today.

5 May

So he set off and went to his father. But while he was still far off, his father saw him and was filled with compassion; he ran and put his arms around him and kissed him. (Luke 15:20)

Being able to 'put yourself' in a story helps it to have greater impact. The moment I became a father, this story became more personal. I would do anything for my sons – and I'm sure the vast majority of parents feel similarly about their children. The father's love in this story is unconditional. It is not 'I love you if...', nor 'I love you when...' but 'I love you'. Despite the love we have for our children, parents are still human. We have bad moments when we do not live up to our ideals. The

Father in this passage says to us, and our children: 'I love you'. We have the real and at times challenging task of doing likewise.

6 May

Hannah prayed and said,
'My heart exults in the Lord' (1 Samuel 2:1)

Relationships thrive on communication. If communication dries up, so does the relationship. It is similar with our relationship with God. For our relationship with God to flourish we must pray – the more honest and open, the better. However, unlike other relationships, God will not judge us for not communicating but will wait for us, patiently and lovingly. Hannah's relationship with God is very intimate since 'her heart exults'. In humans, this kind of intimacy would be reserved for a spouse, family member or special friend. May we each take the time to develop such an intimate relationship with God.

7 May

Be merciful just as your Father is merciful.
(Luke 6:36)

It can be so difficult to not judge others – or maybe I'm just speaking for myself! What might it mean to be merciful as God is? Forgiving without having to be asked. Loving others unconditionally including loving in a tender, intimate way as families do, since we are acting like a parent. Seeing the good in others, especially seeing their good intentions when what occurs isn't quite so good. It might also help to remember the benefits of being merciful. It spreads so much positivity rather than being mean-spirited. Such negativity has a physical impact upon all concerned. Some food for thought...

8 May

I give thanks to the Giver of Grace, from whom we
believe, every good and perfect gift proceeds (second
letter of St Clare to Agnes of Prague, quoting
James 1:17)

We know that it is good manners to thank someone who has given you a gift. How much more is this true if I have been given all that I have and all that I am? Such gratitude means I do not get caught up in what *I* can do or what *I* have. These gifts have been given to me 'in trust', like the talents in the parable, to make the most of *for* the community. Those who have great personal wealth can do great good through philanthropy. It is also good to ponder the notion of grace – which is an *unearned* gift. This emphasises that I have done nothing to deserve my gifts. All the more reason to be grateful and make the most of them – for everyone's benefit.

9 May

The Lord is my rock, my fortress, and my deliverer,
my God, my rock in whom I take refuge,
my shield, and the horn of my salvation, my
stronghold. (Psalm 18:2)

Feel like life is a battle? It might be getting out of bed, it might be getting to work, it might be work itself. You might feel like your relationship is a battleground... or maybe it's your family. Having experienced such a feeling, it's good when it stops. Who or what gets you through? The person/people upon whom you can rely. God is always there for me – whether I can sense it or not. And *someone* is always there for me – I just have to look in the right places.

10 *May*

Jesus came and stood among them and said, 'Peace be with you'. (John 20:19)

Peace is a precious commodity; all the more so when we feel like we're in the midst of turmoil. And I suspect that my desire for peace is in direct proportion to the amount of turmoil that I am experiencing. God wants me to be at peace. In my pain and panic, I can forget how to access that peace. I can get peace through prayer – so I need to remember to make time and space for that. I can get peace through being in nature – time and space required. I can get peace through reading the scriptures – as above. I can get peace through a favourite activity – so I must make time. God wants me to be at peace. What am I going to do about it?

11 *May*

What you hold, may you always hold. What you do, may you always do and never abandon. (Second letter of St Clare to Agnes of Prague)

Life throws a variety of challenges at us. The question is: how am I going to respond? Hold firm? Or give up? Clearly, Clare is encouraging Agnes of Prague to hold firm despite having someone in power dissuading her. Holding firm is particularly necessary if you're a woman in the Middle Ages. Prayerful discernment is needed to ensure I am not riding my hobby horse. Agnes was running a hospital for the poor, so that was not at issue. Holding firm is not just necessary for women in the Middle Ages. I've listened to my wife and sisters and female colleagues to know that it is still a reality. May we come to a time when good people can do what is right without interference. And may I not be an obstacle to that...

12 May

Jesus straightened up and said to her, 'Woman, where are they? Has no one condemned you?' She said, 'No one, sir'. And Jesus said, 'Neither do I condemn you. Go your way, and from now on do not sin again'.
(John 8:10-11)

Sex sells. Humans can frequently wish to hear about people's relationships, including the 'gory details'. We can be so quick to leap to judgment. This story masterfully portrays the compassion of Jesus – for which the Gospel of Luke is well known which is why this passage has been associated with that Gospel. While Mosaic Law (Leviticus 20:12) says the woman *and* man should be stoned to death, there is no mention of the man in this story. But Jesus does not condone what the woman has done – he just does not condemn her. Simply put: 'learn from your mistake'. Tellingly, Jesus does not go along with the stoning – but calls those present to a higher law. The higher law of love – toward which we are all called.

13 May

From the city the dying groan,
and the throat of the wounded cries for help;
yet God pays no attention to their prayer. (Job 24:12)

Perception is a powerful thing. It shapes and colours our reality. This is true whether we see the world in a negative or a positive way. There is no doubt that there is plenty of difficulty in the world – people struggling to make ends meet, others struggling to stay alive. Saying that God pays no attention to their prayer can imply a belief in a 'magical' God – who always fixes problems. What happens when the problem is not fixed? Maybe God pays attention to their prayer by the hearts that are moved to work for change or are moved to ease the plight of those in difficulty. We need to be aware that prayer is not always answered in the way we're expecting.

14 May

He will regard the prayer of the destitute,
and will not despise their prayer. (Psalm 102:17)

As human beings, we can be caught up in appearances. If someone is dirty, smelly or generally unkempt, then we can judge that they have done something wrong. Their reality could be due to a corporate redundancy, mental illness or other factors outside of their control. God doesn't judge as we do. God doesn't judge them or their prayer. God thirsts to be in relationship with us because God knows (before we do) how important and life-giving prayer can be for us. Like a loving parent, God wants the best for us. No matter what we each look like, we are members of God's creation, made in God's image and should be accorded dignity and respect.

15 May

Mothers

Link to our past
Give birth to us
And our future
Share their wisdom
And those of their line
As well as precious memories.
All the gestures
All the sayings
All the laughter
All the love
Made manifest
In countless ways
Across the years.
'Thank you'
Hardly seems enough
But it's a good start
Along with accepting the baton
To create nurturing, inclusive communities
In our turn

16 May

*But whenever you pray, go into your room and shut
the door and pray to your Father who is in secret;
and your Father who sees in secret will reward you.
(Matthew 6:5)*

At least in part, this passage is about spiritual maturity.
Why am I praying? To be seen doing the right thing?
To get the pat on the back as good girl/boy? The reason
for prayer is to enhance our relationship with God.
What others do or do not see is immaterial, so long as
we are building our relationship with God. Building our
relationship with God helps us to grow as individuals –
to be calm and centred. Prayer helps us to realise both
what does not matter and what truly does matter. Prayer
helps us to see our connection, not just to God, but to all
of humanity. This is some reward!

17 May

*The fruit of the Spirit is love, joy, peace, patience,
kindness, generosity, faithfulness, gentleness, and self-
control. (Galatians 5:22-23)*

At the first Pentecost, the followers of Jesus were
empowered by the Holy Spirit. I think that it's an
expression of our humanity when we expect the Holy
Spirit will *only* manifest in an obvious way. This passage
reminds us that we can also be guided by the Holy Spirit
in more gentle, relational ways – that may be more long-

lasting. Each of the fruits of the Spirit influences others positively in an everyday way.

Exemplifying the fruits of the Spirit is something we can each cultivate. As we scan the list we see that those gifts are good for the person who possesses them but they are *meant* to be shared. The gifts of the Spirit build community so that we more closely resemble our triune God in whose image we are made – freely giving of ourselves to others.

18 May

Abide in me as I abide in you. Just as the branch cannot bear fruit by itself unless it abides in the vine, neither can you unless you abide in me. (John 15:4)

This passage flies in the face of our individualistic world yet goes to the heart of Christianity. The body of Christ is greater than the sum of its parts. Connected with others you counterbalance my shortcomings and vice versa. I hope and pray that you've had the experience of a vital Christian community at work as I have. It's a wondrous sight! What sets us apart from other groups is that we are gathered in Christ. We have found, or are in the process of finding, that imitating Jesus in a life of love, compassion, prayer and doing for those in need gives life to me... and us. This focus on a higher power takes me away from my selfish concerns and redirects me to utilise my God-given gifts in order to further build this body of Christ.

19 May

There are those who draw attention to themselves
But not my gentle friend
Who quietly stirs the hearts
Of those with good will
Who prompts the shy smile
Who prompts the reticent student
To ask a question
Who helps our hearts
Blaze against injustice
Who helps us see the good
In others and ourselves
Who can use the words of a man
Full of failings
To help another
Glimpse their heart's longings

O come Holy Spirit?
No
Our gentle friend
Is already with us.
Am I paying attention?

20 May

Seven men were gathered
Singing in Croatian
A capella
With a rich tone and harmonies
Accentuated
By their choice of space
With its acoustics
And ambience
In Diocletian's palace in Split

What moved me to tears?
The ability of music
To share passion
And connect souls
In a moment, uncapturable
For which one must be
Present

Or as Keats put it:
'Truth is beauty, beauty truth
that's all ye know on earth
and all ye need to know'

21 May

While I was still young, before I went on my travels,
 I sought wisdom openly in my prayer.
 (Ecclesiasticus 51:13)

Wisdom can be earned or learned in a number of ways. It is interesting to reflect upon Wisdom as a name for the Holy Spirit. Also, that the Holy Spirit 'will guide you into the truth' (John 16:13). Sound like wisdom to you? Frequently, wisdom comes from reflecting upon one's experience. Did I do the right thing? What might I do differently? Young people can be wise, but it is less common. More likely, wisdom is the end result of a process of listening for and being open to God's prompts in my life. Such a process is enhanced through prayer.

22 May

Now during those days he went out to the mountain
to pray; and he spent the night in prayer to God.
(Luke 6:12)

It is easy to get fired up about getting things done but our actions will have a more positive impact if they have a well thought-out direction. This is part of the importance of prayer that centres us and allows us to sort our delusions from a clear-eyed vision. Prayer helps us to see the plank in our own eye as well as the needs of others and where we can help. Jesus prayed to maintain his relationship with the Father and to give his teaching and his actions clear direction. This was an effective strategy for him! As disciples of Jesus, we also need to pray – whatever our reservations or feelings of being 'unworthy'. Such thoughts and feelings are part of 'the plank' we must remove – to be whole and holy.

23 May

They devour widows' houses and for the sake of appearance say long prayers. (Mark 12:40)

For those of us who are trying to stand for something, the hypocrite is galling. External battles are one matter but when some can be pointed to as saying one thing and doing another, it is all the more challenging. This is intensified when such people hold positions of power, which brings us back to this passage. Prayer is intended to connect us to God, allowing us to see our connection with others and make us better people. So we then look to help others with their burden – not add to it. We should be free to display our faith, primarily through good works, but our faith should never be 'for show'. That is theatre, not faith.

24 May

When Jesus also had been baptised and was praying,
the heaven was opened, and the Holy Spirit descended
upon him in bodily form like a dove. And a voice
came from heaven, 'You are my Son, the Beloved'.
(Luke 3:21-22)

It takes more than three hundred years to pass after the writing of this Gospel before the belief in the Trinity is settled. Yet, in words and images, we have here a basis for that belief. Importantly, there is a loving relationship between the three persons that is accessed through prayer. This is both a relationship to aspire to but also one to which we humans can relate. We can relate to it because as parents we love our children (at least in our good moments!) We aspire to the Trinitarian relationship because there is a constancy we humans can find difficult to maintain amidst the hurly-burly of daily life. Crucially, this is the God in whose image we are made – a God who *is* relationship.

25 May

Lord, teach us to pray. (Luke 11:1)

To learn and grow, you must be open. The disciples are ready and asking Jesus to teach them. Importantly, the disciples acknowledge their need to be closer to God, which lies behind being taught to pray. Growing closer to God in prayer is an important part of the faith journey. The disciples might be grasping their need for prayer in the context of their ministry. They have also watched Jesus go off to pray at significant moments and for lengthy periods. They can see what Jesus does and how vital prayer is to him. They want to know some of Jesus' 'secret' as he has such authority. May we each continue to learn in prayer and about prayer.

26 May

Then he withdrew from them about a stone's throw, knelt down, and prayed, 'Father, if you are willing, remove this cup from me; yet, not my will but yours be done'. (Luke 22:42)

Pray in a trying moment. This is one point of Jesus' example to take from this passage. But more than that we see Jesus' utter humanity laid bare. Who would want to endure agony if given a way out? That requires a level of thought that is not always easy while you're in pain. Jesus then turns it all on its head. Despite the pain, he acknowledges that his death is part of a divine plan. In doing so, Jesus glimpses a vision more grand. Or, as a wise Irish nun once told me: 'God's will for you is what you would do, deep down'. By accepting his death, Jesus crowned his life with integrity. This integrity speaks more eloquently than an individual's desires – but maybe not as loudly.

27 May

*You shall not follow a majority in wrongdoing; when
you bear witness in a lawsuit, you shall not side with
the majority so as to pervert justice. (Exodus 23:2)*

I find it difficult to imagine what it is like to have your
humanity, your culture minimised, disregarded – an
object of scorn and derision at worst, patronising
platitudes for much of the rest of the time. Beginning
with the legal fiction of Australia being *terra nullius*
(land that belonged to no-one), Aboriginal people and
culture have had a difficult journey. One of the very
few referenda that has been passed by the Australian
people, the 1967 referendum recognising the humanity
and thus voting rights of Aboriginals, was a significant
step forward. That difficult journey continues.

28 May

*We must help each person to live more and more
clearly and deeply from an inner confidence of being
loved by God just as they are. (Jean Vanier)*

There are so many factors that can dent my confidence
of being loved by God. The biggest of those is self-
judgment. I can have an internal scoreboard of all my
peccadilloes and I don't 'measure up'. I can also be quick
to internalise other's judgment of me: 'there I go again!'
In trying to work with or help others, if everything
doesn't turn out right immediately 'why did I think I
could help?' Then, when I hear the words of scripture

about suffering or final judgment, I can assume that is my fate. Rather, like everything God created, I was made good. Our belief is that God is love. Story after story in the Gospels show us the example of Jesus' love and mercy and compassion. Step by halting step if I am to truly live the Gospel, I choose to embrace God who has never stopped embracing me – and in so doing embrace myself and my God-given goodness.

29 May

There are moments
In life
That you want
To bottle
Precious moments
Where feelings are
Heightened.
It could be
A wedding
A birth
Magnificent scenery
Or something
As quotidian
As seeing
Your love
Or having dinner
With your family
The trick is
To savour
This grace.

30 May

Now there are varieties of gifts, but the same Spirit;
and there are varieties of services, but the same Lord.
(1 Corinthians 12:4-5)

We don't need to live for very long to realise that there is a
limit to our gifts and abilities. Sometimes, unfortunately,
what we *can't* do is brought into sharper focus that what
we can do. Rather, it is better to focus on my talents and
what I can offer my community. Importantly, the focus
should be on God as the giver of all gifts. We each have
a part to play that only we can. Hopefully, life will teach
me of the beauty of working together – whether it is
team sport or group work or some other opportunity.
That moment is a chance for my eyes to be opened to the
wisdom and joy of our interdependence.

31 May

The Lord is near to the broken-hearted
and saves the crushed in spirit. (Psalm 34:18)

It is easy to feel isolated and alone in our pain. Some
may feel or have been excluded – doubling the hurt.
This is precisely when we need to be comforted. God is
present with us always. As spirit, in ways that we can't
comprehend. God is also present in each of us – this
is the power of the Incarnation. God is also present in
everyone around us, especially when they are moved by
compassion and love to care for those in need. It might
be a piece of scripture or the beauty of God's creation

that might lift a person. It could be the divine spark within that keeps them going. Someone who feels alone in their pain will be reached powerfully by someone who acts as God's heart and hands, as it reminds them they are always in community.

JUNE

133

1 June

The cold north wind blows,
  and ice freezes on the water;
it settles on every pool of water,
  and the water puts it on like a breastplate.
(Ecclesiasticus 43:20)

Humans are so used to living with the illusion of control that our lack of control over the weather can annoy us. This is particularly so if the weather is bleak, cold and trying. Thus, winter is rarely embraced, including in Australia where the temperature rarely drops to freezing. From an ecological perspective, winter is an important part of the natural cycle where living things gather their energies for the burst of spring. We would appreciate spring less if there was no winter. Nature teaches humans an important lesson in winter: retreat, reflect, take time for yourself. Almost like God intended it!

2 June

You shall not pervert the justice due to your poor in
their lawsuits. (Exodus 23:6)

It is only a narrow, legalistic mindset that would say that land that has been occupied for generations by your people *isn't* yours. But based in a paternalistic and patronising English legal system designed for English culture, Aboriginals were consistently denied their land rights, including down the barrel of a gun. It took a determined man, Eddie Mabo, using his own resources and those of willing others, to finally win the landmark legal battle that confirmed what he knew – the land belonged to his people. May I not be so bound by culture as to ignore justice.

3 June

Waves surging
Made more boisterous
By an icy wind

Grin on the face of a passer by
Sharing joy
In our kelpie's delight
Of retrieving the ball

Pale stump of a rainbow

The morning's crowning glory
A cloud, brilliant white
Rimmed in the sun's gold
Topped by a dazzling
Shaft of light

This is living

4 June

Preach the Gospel always. Use words when necessary.
(St Francis of Assisi)

How will those who have not heard the Good News learn about it? Over the centuries, missionary efforts have taken different shapes. Rather than a verbal preaching of the word, Francis is speaking of the example of integrity. To lead a life so compassionate, so loving, so exemplary as to make others wonder: why does she act that way? This gentle, invitational mission acts as God does – slowly, gently, touching hearts. Words eventually cease but the example of a life lovingly lived never ceases. The lives of Francis, Clare and other saints are proof.

5 June

The Lord said, 'Obey my voice, and I will be your God,
and you shall be my people'. (Jeremiah 7:23)

To be able to obey God's voice, you have to be listening. This prompts the question: how can I hear God's voice? I can hear God's voice through the scriptures, especially if I read them in a reflective, prayerful way. I can hear God's voice through the teaching of the Church whether that is a homily or the official documents of the Church. I can also hear God's voice through people in my life who guide and direct me in ways that are helpful for *me*. When we obey God's voice, we are guided by an Ultimate

Reality that is bigger than just me. When we obey God's voice, I'm not alone, I'm part of a community who are similarly guided. So, I'm in good company!

6 June

The earth is the Lord's and all that is in it,
the world, and those who live in it. (Psalm 24:1)

Our world can seem to live by 'might is right'. I can have whatever I want and, if I need to use force, then so be it. If there is pollution or damage to the environment of some kind, there can be a shrug of the shoulders: 'you can't make an omelette without breaking some eggs'. A very different paradigm is to see the world as belonging to God – and we just hold it in trust – to care for it now and then pass the stewardship on to the next generation. We see what we do in the world due to the battle of paradigms. Each of us must determine where our heart truly lies on this matter. We must also review if there is a gap between what I say and what I do.

7 *June*

For where your treasure is, there also will your heart
be. (Matthew 6:21)

Who or what is your 'starting place'? For me, it's my
relationship with my wife. Her daily, practical love
and support is steadfast – I can always depend upon it.
When I am unsure about what to do, her wise and gentle
counsel allows me to see the direction I should take. Our
jokes and laughs together are a safety valve amidst life's
constant demands. Together we have shared the joy and
pain of raising two sons who mean so much to both of
us. When I hold her in my arms, she is all that matters
at that moment – and despite whatever else is occurring
everything seems 'right'. In our perfectly imperfect way,
we are God's love for each other. May you be similarly
blessed.

8 *June*

Another influential musician
Has died
There should be sadness
At the passing
Of another human life
But what's left behind?
Music

Whether it's the music of
John Lennon

Jimi Hendrix
Kurt Cobain
Now, Chris Cornell
Stevie Ray Vaughan
Howlin' Wolf
Muddy Waters
B.B. King
Or hundreds of others
Music can touch humans deeply
And despite the different ways
It can affect people
Music provides such
A passionate connection
Among those who live for it

Music excites
It warms
It moves
It connects

One heck of a gift
To leave behind

9 June

Lead me in your truth, and teach me. (Psalm 25:5)

Like many things in life, coming to know the truth is a journey. It is as much an inward as a physical journey. I must embrace the truth about myself – my shortcomings and my gifts. In so doing I might grow in compassion for others on their journey – and see our connectedness. I also must let go of the notion of truth being a kind of destination. This journey is an unfolding as much as it is a shedding. As I come to grasp what is true, in me and around me, I also let go of some of the things to which I previously clung. Thus as we grow in the truth, we are also being taught by the God who knows us and our needs.

10 June

To you, O Lord, I lift up my soul. (Psalm 25:1)

It is so easy to be caught or stuck in the worries and cares of daily life. Whether it is arguments, bills to pay, deadlines or the like, we can feel bogged down. Thus the psalmist expresses the human desire to escape what weighs us down. This passage also expresses a prayerful disposition, 'to be where God is'. The counterpoint to that is our faith that believes that God is always *with us*. Thus in part it is an issue of perception. What steps do I need to take to 'be where God is'? It might be taking a breath or stepping back from an activity or interaction.

It might be factoring in some reflective, prayerful time where we can 'hand things over' – before starting again. Or as simple and powerful as noticing a sunrise, natural beauty, a baby or a smile.

11 June

He looked up and saw rich people putting their gifts into the treasury; he also saw a poor widow put in two small copper coins. He said, 'Truly I tell you, this poor widow has put in more than all of them; for all of them have contributed out of their abundance, but she out of her poverty has put in all she had to live on'.
(Luke 21:1-4)

We live in an age that promotes 'being seen'. There are sufficient contemporary examples of this passage not to labour the point – people with significant means being seen to do the right thing. Having said that, the charitable sector is well organised and there is an end to how much each person can give. It is up to each person to decide. Then as now we need to not confuse amount with capacity. A significant part of this passage is about judging – 'do not judge' is the gold standard. Human nature being what it is, judging is still likely to happen. Thus the excellent advice of 1 Samuel 16:7: 'do not see as humans see, humans look at appearances. God looks at the heart'.

12 June

Divided tongues, as of fire, appeared among them,
and a tongue rested on each of them. All of them were
filled with the Holy Spirit. (Acts 2:3-4)

Jesus' promise of the Holy Spirit upon his departure is
made good at Pentecost. The symbolism signifies that
God is always with us. This occurs most powerfully when
we are part of a faith community that prays, works and
discerns together. In that situation, I can discover and
utilise my God-given gifts to build up the community.
In this passage, *each* of them was gifted but it was a
community exercise. My giftedness is not *for* me. My
talents are not for self-aggrandisement or to boost my
ego. This giving away of self is the Holy Spirit guiding us
into the truth about our greatness in faith when we are
connected to each other and to God.

13 June

Spending time in foreign countries
It's easy to focus
On the differences –
In language
Customs
Bank notes

Yet, we have a common currency
In our humanity
Seen in children

Their joy and delight in the simple
Such as dancing and singing
Frequently on tip-toes
Their agency in pressing buttons –
To cross the road
Or wherever they can get their hands on them!
Their mimicry of adult behaviour
Which can raise an amusing
As well as uncomfortable mirror
To adults

Thus we adults have a choice:
Do we focus on agency
As well as joy and delight
And pay attention
To the mirror
Held up for us?
Or do we stumble
Along dark paths
That lead to
Distrust, division
And destruction?

14 June

*He said therefore, 'What is the kingdom of God like?
And to what should I compare it? It is like a mustard
seed that someone took and sowed in the garden; it
grew and became a tree, and the birds of the air made
nests in its branches" (Luke 13:18-19)*

Describing the kingdom of God is very difficult. It is
never a place and isn't really tangible. This is why Jesus
uses figures of speech and parables to describe it. Here,
it is about the flourishing that can occur. What can seem
small and insignificant can, like a mustard seed, grow
into something that is not only substantial but enriching
for others. The kingdom of God comes through
justice and right relationships. The bonds of a strong
community are visible only through people's behaviour.
I hope that, like me, you've witnessed the extraordinary
flourishing that can occur in such a community.

15 June

Hail Mary, full of grace...

I'm not sure how much Mary has been credited with
strength. To observe your son and his difficulties during
his public ministry then watch his humiliating death –
and to stay the course? *There's* strength and there must
have been grace to keep her going. She had received
inklings along the way of what was to come but her faith
during all that time *is* remarkable. Then, after Jesus'

death, to be a rock to help keep the dream alive in the fledgling community – further grace. And so it is with gifts. While Mary was gifted to do as she did, a further grace is the example she provides for us today.

16 June

He said, 'Go out and stand on the mountain before the Lord, for the Lord is about to pass by'. Now there was a great wind, so strong that it was splitting mountains and breaking rocks in pieces before the Lord, but the Lord was not in the wind; and after the wind an earthquake, but the Lord was not in the earthquake; and after the earthquake a fire, but the Lord was not in the fire; and after the fire a sound of sheer silence. When Elijah heard it, he wrapped his face in his mantle and went out and stood at the entrance of the cave. (1 Kings 19:11-13)

God works differently to humans. Rather than being in the obvious place or manifestation, God was present in the 'sound of sheer silence'. It is also about having eyes and ears to see and hear God in the less 'obvious' place. The beauty of the *New Revised Standard Version* translation is that it is an indication to us of where we might find God, especially in prayer. Silence is easily masked by sounds – such as the 'white noise' of modern life. Thus I need to be alert and listen for the silence so that I can celebrate and acknowledge God's presence in my life – especially those times and places I least expect.

17 June

The Lord takes delight in his people. (Psalm 149:4)

We take delight in those we love. It might be our children – at whatever age and stage they are at. It could be a partner or spouse and my desire just to be with them or be present while they 'do their thing'. And so God loves each of us and takes delight in my unique unrepeatable identity. God loves me for being me. Would that we each loved ourselves in the way God loves us! Since God takes delight in each of us, we do well to follow that example to love others to the best of our ability. May we see our connectedness rather than our division and see that together we are God's people.

18 June

The Lord does not see as mortals see; they look on the outward appearance, but the Lord looks on the heart. (1 Samuel 16:7)

In one way or another, humans spend a lot of time making themselves look good. Some self-respect in your general appearance is healthy. But others have crossed the line to obsession such that it is 'good for the economy'. It is easy to be seduced into this vortex – rather than 'looking at the heart'. Looking at the heart I might ask: What is this person's behaviour towards others? Are they kind? Compassionate? Do they help those in need? How does this person speak about others? Themselves? And while I'm at it – I can ask the same questions of myself.

19 June

Father, hallowed be your name. (Luke 11:2)

Saying God's name is holy is important – living that belief is even more so. And how can I live that God's name is holy? One way is through prayer – since God is holy I want to be in relationship with God. Another way that I live that God's name is holy is through my relationships. I am created in God's image and through the Trinity, God is relationship; thus my relationships are intended to be marked by compassion and respect for the dignity of each person. When I respect God's creation through my appreciation of nature and use of resources, I also live that God's name is holy.

20 June

Your kingdom come. (Luke 11:2)

What can sound pious is very practical. Why? St Paul tells us that God's reign comes through righteousness that is better translated as right relationships and justice. Where there is justice, those who are on the margins are cared for. Where there are right relationships, then everyone is respected. Thus God's reign comes through the quality of our relationships. This is not a surprise since the Trinity reveals that God is relationship: Father, Son and Spirit. So God's reign will come through relationships that demonstrate dignity, respect and compassion. Powerful and practical.

21 June

We are each caught
In a tapestry
Of love.

God, who is the love
Of our parents,
Worked through them
And in them
To love us into life
Adding our thread
To the whole.

But the tapestry
Isn't static.
Threads respond
To each other
In harmony
Or not.
Inasmuch as we are
Loving and authentic
We bring colour and beauty
To the tapestry.

In God's time
Our threads
May coalesce
Thereby bringing
Other threads

Into being.
We nurture those threads
And others,
The warp and the weft
Aiding the master weaver.
Sharing love
Sharing God

22 June

*I am the Lord your God, who brought you out of the
land of Egypt, out of the house of slavery; you shall
have no other gods before me. (Exodus 20:2)*

How easy it is to be seduced by other 'gods'! We can say
we believe and engage in faith practices – whilst also
harbouring other beliefs that run counter to God. We
might make a god out of money – focusing too much on
its accumulation or on spending it. We might make a
god out of power and control – disregarding the feelings
of others. We might make a god out of possessions
and their accumulation. There are a myriad of other
obsessions that could claim too much of our time or
energy. If my focus is on God, then my behaviour will
focus on promoting right relationships and justice. My
focus will *not* be on me. I will be grateful to God for all
that I have. I will show that gratitude by focusing on the
needs of others.

23 June

Give us each day our daily bread. (Luke 11:3)

What do we need to survive? We need somewhere to sleep that is safe and warm. We need food and water. Thus 'daily bread' should be taken in its literal sense of necessary food. I think 'daily bread' could also mean all the related things needed both to survive and thrive. This is particularly important to remember for those of us (like me) whose daily needs are comfortably met. The Our Father is a communal prayer. Am I remembering my communal responsibilities? Am I caring for the physical needs of others? Am I caring for the emotional needs of others by engaging in right relationships?

24 June

And forgive us our sins. (Luke 11:4)

As humans we can bear a burden of guilt – sometimes for many years. I need to believe in a God who forgives – so that I can eventually forgive myself. I need a God who constantly reminds me: 'I loved you into life. You were created by love for love'. I need this reminder as I obsess over details and judge myself harshly. I need this reminder so that my fingers that tightly clutch my mistakes might slowly open. Then my hands are open to receive God's love – which comes in many forms. Then I am more open to and compassionate with others. God's gentle love knocks at the door of my heart – reminding me, 'I've already forgiven you'. May I open the door...

25 June

For we ourselves forgive everyone indebted to us.
(Luke 11:4)

Think of the countless times this prayer is recited both publicly and privately. Do I think about what I'm saying? Do I actually reflect upon what the prayer is expecting of me? I expect to be forgiven but do I forgive others? That definitely fits in 'easier said than done'! However, forgiveness serves at least two important purposes. To forgive is to be like God. To forgive is to be a disciple of Jesus. Compassion is part of forgiveness. The act of 'letting go' of past hurts is sound psychology. It allows us to move on and not carry 'baggage'. Such baggage can weigh us down and impede our progress towards wholeness and holiness.

26 June

About to begin
A time of leave
Expectant
Excited.
I've been holding
This in for so long

We've got travel plans
Lots to look forward to
But what will happen?
There's excitement, too,
On the edge of maybe

27 June

Our steps are made firm by the Lord. (Psalm 27:23)

You may know the feeling of being on 'shaky ground'. Being unsure of whether you are saying or doing the right thing. That could be because I've made a mistake OR I am in an excessively judgmental situation. Whatever the reason, feeling tentative like that limits freedom, creativity and authenticity. This is not the full life toward which we are called. It is different if I remember that I was loved into life by God and I act authentically, knowing that my gifts are building up the community which is the body of Christ. Thus God is indeed making my steps firm. Maybe even firm enough to take me away from a toxic environment to one which will give me, and everyone, life.

28 June

And do not bring us to the time of trial. (Luke 11:4)

My experience is that a 'time of trial' is part of life – and we can't always see it coming. We may wish to avoid such times but they will come anyway: 'ready or not'! The more important question is: what is my response to a time of trial? Do I kick the dirt... 'woe is me'? Some trials are difficult and intense – requiring all of my resources. Maybe the best I can do is put one foot in front of the other. But I also need to remember that friends and family are among my 'resources' – who love me and keep me stable and sane. But it is also vital to remember to take time for prayer and reflection. Is there a lesson for me in this trial? Maybe the lesson is to not do it on my own...

29 June   *Saints Peter and Paul*

But when Cephas came to Antioch, I opposed him to his face, because he stood self-condemned; for until certain people came from James, he used to eat with the Gentiles. (Galatians 2:11-12)

There are plenty of Christians who have an idealised view of the early Church. The reality is that there were four centuries of sporadic 'knock 'em down, drag 'em out' fights about doctrine and theology. The beauty of this verse is that it contains two seminal Christian figures – Peter and Paul – at odds with each other. Paul, ever forthright, called Peter out for focusing on externals, rather than the fact that we are all created in the image and likeness of God – and that we are one in the body of Christ. Such wisdom has lessons to teach each of us.

30 June

Blessed are you who are poor,
for yours is the kingdom of God. (Luke 6:20)

They must have thought Jesus was crazy when he uttered these words. To be poor was to be on the outer – that is wretched, *not* blessed. We're told that God's reign comes through justice and right relationships. The poor know their need for others – they *can't* do it by themselves. Whereas those of us who have significant means can be lulled into thinking that we don't need others; indeed, that we don't need God. Thus, blessed are the poor because they know their need to develop relationships with others and don't have material things blinding them into not building relationships. So, God's reign *is* theirs.

JULY

1 July

*You shall not make wrongful use of the name of
the Lord your God. (Exodus 20:7)*

In the world of the Hebrew Scriptures, to 'know
someone's name' implied a close connection, an
intimacy. As with all intimacy, this is not something
to be taken lightly. Intimacy with God is at our deepest
level and implies a commitment to be true to God and
true to ourselves. To be true to God means I am grateful
for everything I am and all that I have as they are God's
gifts to me. To be true to God means that I will respect
my fellow humans as fellow creatures of God. To be true
to God means that I will honour, respect and take care of
the rest of God's creation. Wrongful use of God's name
implies that we have a power over God that is never real.

2 July

*Blessed are you who are hungry now,
for you will be filled. (Luke 6:21)*

Things aren't what they seem! Don't take everything on
face value! When God reigns, justice prevails and so all
of the (still) current inequalities will vanish. This is part
of the themes of the great overturning and compassion
that are seen in Luke's Gospel. As terrible as it is to be
hungry, there are worse situations. Such as having plenty
of food but not having 'enough'. Having a spiritual or
existential hole that nothing can fill. Again, those who

are hungry know they cannot do it on their own and so build relationships. Their needs are simple... not never-ending. Those in hunger are an opportunity for God's grace – to touch the hearts and hands of those with the political or physical means to help.

3 July

I stand dry
Watching
This watery spectacle
Of driving rain
As it drenches
The garden
Whose green bushes
Were lapping up
This bounty
Slender branches
Of a deciduous tree
With last vestiges
Of gold and brown
Allowed rivulets
To course down
Its trunk

This ordinary scene
Jolted me
With its grace

4 July

Remember the sabbath day, and keep it holy.
(Exodus 20:8)

I find it easy to be driven so I need to make myself stop. Part of the Sabbath is to rest in order to pause from work. With the connectedness and intrusion of media in the contemporary world, that is no simple matter! Yet I am fully myself only when I pause, giving thanks to our God who loves the whole world into life. Keeping the Sabbath reminds me that it does *not* all depend upon me. Keeping the Sabbath gives me down time I need to keep my work in perspective and to do it well – and be less driven and obsessive. This helps me to use my gifts well and be more whole... and holy.

5 July

Blessed are you who weep now,
for you will laugh. (Luke 6:21)

People who cry are doing so for a reason – it might be because someone I love has passed away; there could be other emotional pain. Often it speaks of a connection of love – but everything is not right. When God's reign is here, we will see as God sees. Because our tears come from a place of love, God will open our eyes to see that 'love never ends'. Any passing or upset will be seen as another form of Love and there will only be joy. So we will laugh – maybe even at ourselves for not having enough faith.

6 July

*Blessed are you when people hate you, and when they
exclude you, revile you, and defame you on account of
the Son of Man. (Luke 6:22)*

If it happens to you, it is no picnic. Being excluded,
reviled, defamed on account of your faith might have
you asking God about the justice of it all. Yet this is
the situation for many over the centuries. One way of
looking at it is: 'you know you're doing a good job when
you're strongly attacked'. You are a person of integrity,
living the Gospel – which comforts the afflicted and
afflicts the comfortable. However, we do have feelings.
It would be crucial to feel that you had *someone* in your
corner. Yes, we know we always have God but we are
flesh and blood and need support.

7 July

Honour your father and your mother. (Exodus 20:12)

Depending upon one's point in the ageing process, this commandment can be self-evident, even easy – or it can be challenging. Maybe circumstances due to your parents' flaws such as absence or addiction might also make the commandment challenging. Part of it is about one's perspective. When I became a parent I became more immediately aware of all that was done for me as a child – and so I have expressed my gratitude to my mother. While my father was an alcoholic, I value a love of learning and an appreciation of beauty that he passed on to me. Another way of framing the commandment: 'Honour your father and your mother since one day you will become a parent and see it's not so easy'.

8 July

You shall not murder. (Exodus 20:13)

I'm assuming that 99.9% of the population keep this commandment without issue. Digging a little deeper, this commandment is about valuing life as an immense gift from God that you do not have the right to take away. I think the expression 'murderous rage' can be instructive. In such a state you can't see your connectedness to others – only your own pain and hurt. Given that murder is happily not rife in our society it could be helpful to explore the ways that anger hurts me; physically, it can lead to illness; psychologically, it means I only see my perspective and is about 'being right' rather than seeking to build (or re-build) relationships – our God-given task in life.

9 July

When the Spirit of truth comes, he will guide you into
all the truth. (John 16:13)

O how I need the Holy Spirit to guide and direct me! What I love about this passage is that 'the truth' is too much for us to absorb all at once. We need to be guided into truth. This rings true for me in my life – a gradual unfolding. In other words, as I grow as a person I'm able to deal with another part of the truth about myself, others, God, life. Such apprehension of the truth might begin with 'knowing the rules', to 'doing the right thing', to 'getting on with others', to 'watching out for the pitfalls', to 'where I belong'. It might involve re-doing these or other steps before realising 'we are all one in God'. Maybe you can add a few steps of your own?

10 July

You shall not commit adultery. (Exodus 20:14)

This is about damage done – to your integrity, to your spouse and your sexual partner. Giving your deepest intimacy away comes at a cost. Despite what might be said about it being 'a fling', one's sexual partner is not getting 'all' of you, but a hollow shell. Engaging in this behaviour means your integrity has taken a serious blow: you've said one thing and done another. Then there's the spouse who has been betrayed. If the relationship is faltering, deal with it i.e. fix it or end it *before* operating outside the relationship. Making love is the most beautiful way that humans can be to each other. Cheapened in this way, it acts like acid – corroding whatever it touches.

11 July

Lord, make me an instrument of your peace. (St Francis of Assisi)

This first line of the prayer of St Francis honours God as the author of peace and implies that peace is a desirable commodity. This line has the focus of bringing peace *for* others – so it begins by looking to be of service. In asking to be 'an instrument of your peace', I am to be used by God to bring the peace that belongs to God. Such peace is deep and all encompassing. Human life has always had distractions but there are so many in today's world that the deep peace from God is particularly timely and needed. We each need peace to discern the right course of action, to block out the white noise and feel whole.

12 July

You shall not steal. (Exodus 20:15)

Stealing might occur due to poverty – like my chimney sweep ancestor who was transported to Australia for stealing a side of bacon – but that is very different. Taking what is not yours isn't just wrong because you've harmed someone else. Stealing also says that what you have is not 'enough'. Feeling that who you are and what you have *is* enough is vital to self-acceptance, which quietens a restless yearning. Stealing disrespects God as the giver of all gifts both because your gifts are not enough and you're taking what another has been gifted. Stealing wounds your integrity and any relationship you might have.

13 July

Where there is hatred, let me sow love. (St Francis of Assisi)

Hatred is a strong word – and yet there is sufficient evidence of its existence in our society – let alone those that are wracked by enmity and division. Hatred might be caused by old wounds that could be cultural or religious. Love is sown gently, patiently, through actions, words and relationships. By sowing love, I am providing an example, an opportunity to live differently. By sowing love, I'm encouraging others to see that our shared humanity is greater than anything that divides us. By sowing love, I allow people to see that it is possible to let go of past hurts. By sowing love, others might glimpse a chance for hope, joy and happiness.

14 July

When we think
Of the moon
It is likely to be
In its radiant fullness
Which can provide
So much light
On a clear evening.
Today
The moon
Revealed
A shy sliver

As it rose
Against the early morning sky
The sliver
Was orange
Reflecting
The not-yet-risen sun
Such a sliver
Speaks to me
The most.
Ethereal
Achingly beautiful.

Moments pass
I want to experience
That beauty
Again
But
Somehow
In a clear sky
The moon is invisible
Shy?
Just waiting
The right moment
To next reveal
Another side
Of your glory

15 July

You shall not bear false witness against your neighbour. (Exodus 20:16)

There are various forms of lying. But to say publicly something that you know to be untrue about someone? I can't get my head around that. I can only imagine that such behaviour is fuelled by anger, jealousy or revenge. None of those is a helpful starting point for action. And it is not solely about the person being wronged. There is an old saying: 'the person who throws mud loses ground'. Such behaviour means that one is diminishing one's integrity and credibility. There is also the likelihood of damaging relationships. There are more helpful ways (for all concerned) to deal with your feelings.

16 July

You shall not covet your neighbour's house; you shall not covet your neighbour's wife, or male or female slave, or ox, or donkey, or anything that belongs to your neighbour. (Exodus 20: 17)

The 'shopping list' seems designed to 'cover all the bases' – for the mind looking for loopholes. Granted that in today's world, speaking of one person 'belonging' to another does not sit well. That aside, coveting the gifts of another is *not* criminal. However, by coveting, I imply that what I have is not enough (and thus I am not enough?). I disrespect the person whose gifts I covet *and* I disrespect God as the giver of all gifts. Thus coveting can damage my relationships and get in the way of building healthy relationships. Why? I'm focused on things not people.

17 July

Where there is injury, pardon. (St Francis of Assisi)

Forgiveness is precious. Without it I can cling on to past hurts – those I've caused as well as those I've suffered. Without forgiveness, I am 'stuck' and any other interactions or relationships are affected or coloured in some way by those past hurts. Without forgiveness of the hurts I've caused I will feel less human, less worthy than those around me. Without forgiveness of the hurts I've suffered, I will feel less human, wondering if I brought it upon myself OR I may be stuck in my anger. Forgiveness is the circuit breaker that allows us to move forward, to live life to the full. Forgiveness also allows me to see that everyone else has past hurts – and so compassion grows.

18 July

O Lord, who may abide in your tent?
Who may dwell on your holy hill?
Those who walk blamelessly, and do what is right,
and speak the truth from their heart. (Psalm 15:1-2)

Like me, you might think this is a tall order! Yet, for me
to be *with* God, I need to choose to live in this way that
isn't just about 'being good' but that builds community.
If I choose to behave differently, then I am choosing not
to abide with God. God hasn't moved – I have! Instead,
if my focus is on building community then I want to do
the right thing by others and foster strong relationships.
Importantly, if I am telling the truth and saying positive
things, no one ever gets hurt!

19 July

Sitting in a shopping centre
Whiling away some time
I saw something
Small
Something so
Everyday
That would pass
Without notice
Without comment
But the love that lay
Underneath that gesture
Floored me

Siblings in strollers
Side by side
One pushed by mum
The other by dad
While the siblings held hands
Looking at each other, eyes shining

Love is to be expressed
But true love
Can be so plain
As to go unnoticed

Love shines every day
May we have the eyes to see it
And appreciate its beauty

20 July

Whom must I forgive so that I can teach forgiveness?
(John Baptist De La Salle)

It is easy to focus on the times that I have been aggrieved.
But in the end I can only control my actions and reactions.
So if I am able to follow Jesus' example and be a person of
forgiveness, I can more effectively teach forgiveness by
my example of forgiving others. Psychologically, when I
forgive others my compassion grows. I let go of the hurt
so that it is not a weapon to bludgeon others... or myself.
Compassion and forgiveness enrich relationships;
we have hearts of flesh, not stone. Compassion and
forgiveness bring God's reign closer.

21 July

Where there is despair, hope. (St Francis of Assisi)

To be despairing is to see no positives. It might be because I've encountered the last in a long line of difficulties. Maybe I'm struggling with a massive existential issue. The way back from that point is neither simple nor immediate. To bring hope to someone in despair is to journey with them, gently and consistently reminding them of the positives – mostly in deed. It is pointless to tell someone to 'snap out of it'. I suspect that despair is a form of grief. And grief has stages and takes its own time. By journeying with someone in despair, they may yet come to their own realisation that suffering and death do not have the last word. And that resurrection can occur in many forms.

22 July

Where there is doubt, faith. (St Francis of Assisi)

It has been said that doubt is part of the journey of faith. Doubt can be caused by a number of factors. Doubt may arise because a person's *idea* of God is found to be wanting. Thus the person needs a more spacious way of thinking about God. Doubt may arise because of the failings of church members. The person needs to acknowledge that we all have flaws – without excusing serious misdeeds. Doubts may arise because of a lack of certainty. The person needs to learn to have a lighter grasp since 'certainty' can be a synonym for 'control'. We

come to faith slowly and steadily. Peace and joy follow closely.

23 July

We are not exempt from suffering from others,
because it is not possible for two people to live together
without causing suffering to one another in some
way or other. Because we make others suffer, it is only
right that we should suffer from them in our turn.
(John Baptist De La Salle)

Simply put, *none* of us is perfect. Even when I am doing my very best I make mistakes. I can be thoughtless, rude or hurtful. Thus my rough edges rub up against your rough edges – so there is friction. Importantly, the friction is caused by *both* sides. And the more people involved, the more likely there is to be such friction. If I accept my rough edges, I ought to accept your rough edges. Such acceptance is liberating for all concerned. Such acceptance is the precursor to compassion – and more closely following the way of Christ.

24 July

Where there is darkness, light. (St Francis of Assisi)

While darkness could be a synonym for despair, it might also refer to a time in a person's life when they cannot see. Maybe they cannot see a way forward for themselves in their life. This could be caused by indecision concerning a life choice or something like depression. A person could feel that they're in darkness due to a perceived absence or connection with God – whether that is feeling cut off from God or that God has rejected them (because of a life choice?). To bring light to these situations is to bring love and compassion. Each person is good enough as they are; nothing cuts us off from God's love, mercy and forgiveness which always shine light.

25 July

Where there is sadness, joy. (St Francis of Assisi)

There can be many understandable reasons to be sad. It might be the passing of a loved one – or their departure to live elsewhere. It might be that I feel unappreciated or that my hard work has been for nothing. To stay with these feelings is neither helpful nor right. By staying with a feeling of sadness, I am only looking at the tangible – at what is. Rather I need to see what might be. Teilhard de Chardin said that 'joy is the infallible sign of the presence of God'. Someone's departure might be to the next phase of their life with personal growth. Maybe my work is to sow – and for another to harvest.

26 July

In order to be of service in our Institute, which aims at helping to establish peace in countries and within people, we must have a knowledge of God and great zeal. We must act with tact and humility, and with no self-interest...If everywhere we try to be angels of peace, we shall indeed be clothed in the spirit of St Francis. (Helene de Chappotin)

An angel is a messenger from God – which means that *my* message is not the one to be shared. This peace I am desiring to spread requires me to 'have knowledge of God' – which comes through prayer and reflection on my experience. It also requires zeal – this is not for the half-hearted! To continue to live with zeal I must be constantly seeking connections with God, too. Likewise, God's message of peace will only be spread if I have tact and humility. I know I'm a 'work in progress' in that regard! Finally, no self-interest. This is not about me or my ideas or improving *my* situation. In that way, the message is not confused with the messenger. What greater reward than fostering peace!

27 July

Lost in a fog of negativity
I am jolted
When I look up
At the blue sky
A tree's slender, naked branches
Festooned with sparrows
Perched in them

I am struck
By the earthy everyday
Joy and wonder

This salve
Reminds me
Of what truly matters

28 July

*O divine Master, grant that I may not so much seek to
be consoled as to console. (St Francis of Assisi)*

We each need to be consoled from time to time – due to
bereavement or another reason. Francis is not saying that
one's feelings do not matter. By *seeking* to console I'm not
ignoring my feelings, nor is it about power. Rather, by
seeking to console, I'm looking to grow my empathy and
compassion. By seeking to console, I am not stuck in my
feelings, I'm looking to go out to another. By seeking to
console, I am looking to build relationships. By seeking

to console, I am also acknowledging the human need and God-given dignity of another – I am honouring the Incarnation.

29 July

When giving an opinion, you must be careful not to maintain it stubbornly, for you should not be so sure of your ideas as to think them incontrovertible. (John Baptist De La Salle)

I need to remind myself about my motivation. I am a disciple of Jesus. I am here to spread the Gospel through my actions and my words. I need to remind myself of my flaws – so that I remember that I only have part of the story. I can and should share my opinion – based in my experience and understanding – but I still have much to learn. And others can teach me if I shut up and listen! I know I'm not the only person who 'likes to be right'. My experience has shown me that it is easy to alienate others in the process. Alienating others is not the Gospel and is not the way of Jesus. Being open to and learning from others builds community.

30 July

To be understood as to understand. (St Francis of Assisi)

To be understood is great – but the focus is just on me. Whereas if I understand, my focus is outward. If I understand, then I can be more compassionate. To understand is to see connections, discern nuances and know a situation as it is. To understand means I am less likely to 'put my foot in it' as I will understand someone's 'back story' including the stories of pain that we each carry. If I understand, I can build relationships. Relationships that are right and just and so bring God's reign a little closer.

31 July

Pride makes us forgetful of our eternal interests. It causes us to neglect totally the care of our soul. (John Baptist De La Salle)

A healthy self-belief is important – pride is when that self-belief is over-inflated. Pride leads me to think it is all about me and how awesome I am. Pride blinds me to my faults and so I neglect my inner work. Pride makes a person difficult to live with, affecting others. Pride also diminishes the contributions others can and should make, as part of the body of Christ. All because an ego takes over. As is said 'pride comes before a fall'. Pride has been rich fodder for playwrights like Shakespeare in plays such as *Macbeth*. Pride is tragic – but avoidable.

AUGUST

1 August

To be loved as to love. (St Francis of Assisi)

We all have needs. For secure attachment and a healthy upbringing, we need to be loved. As an adult, we still need to be loved by our partner and family, so that we can deal with what life throws at us. But to love is to participate in God's creative work. To love brings people and things to life, building relationships. To love art, music, architecture or gardening is to embrace that activity, get the most from it and to share that love with others – sharing the joy. To love people is to see their giftedness – sometimes when they can't see it themselves – and so guide them to be all that they can be.

2 August

You must be particularly careful not to be lax with regard to your spiritual exercises. (John Baptist De La Salle)

It is easy to be busy. In fact, it can be both comforting *and* a badge of honour to be busy: 'I'm so needed, so important. I'm busy'. In reality, my work will be more effective if I take time in prayer and contemplation. Such activity helps me to regain my centre – including a sense of peace and purpose. This makes it more likely that my actions will align with my purpose. Also, these spiritual exercises are not to receive 'praise for being good'. They are good for me and help me to discern how to act with integrity on a daily basis

3 August

I was gardening in my front yard
And a three year old girl
And her parents walked past.
Dad was pushing the girl's bike
Mum was pushing the younger sibling in a stroller.
The girl stood up straight
And proudly proclaimed to me
As her helmet topped her outfit
That she was riding a two-wheeled bike.
I agreed that this was an excellent achievement.
We continued our exchange
In a similarly forthright and earnest fashion
For a few more moments.
What struck me
As I thanked her parents for this grace
Is that children grow and develop
Because of the love from their parents.
This couple's love was on display, in spades,
And was a wonder to witness.

4 August

For it is in giving that we receive. (St Francis of Assisi)

At face value, this can seem counter-intuitive. However, further thought reveals the deep truth and wisdom behind this statement. When I give to others, I receive the rosy glow of a job well done. When I give to others, I'm doing my best to live my faith. When I give to others, I empower and support them. When I give to others, there is a deep satisfaction – no thanks are necessary. When I give to others, I'm doing what my gifts were intended for – to be given away and so build community. A community that is focused on 'what I can give' is a place of care, support, growth – and love.

5 August

And it is in dying that we are born to eternal life. (St Francis of Assisi)

There are so many things that are regarded as 'important' in life but they are all extensions of the ego, my *false* self. My ego defines myself *against* others – am I more powerful? Have more possessions? My happiness lies in an opposite direction. If I die to myself, I see more of the big picture than just my selfish concerns. If I die to myself, I am more likely to build right relationships. When I build right relationships, I am building the eternal community, God's reign, where everyone has life and none are less. It begins by dying to self – the way of Francis and the *minores*.

6 August

You should pay attention to your behavior in what concerns not only yourself but others also. For it is impossible to please God if you do not live amicably with others. Nor will you have peace of soul unless you show consideration for those for whom you ought to set a good example. (John Baptist De La Salle)

I know it is easy for me to focus on 'getting the job done'. What I have learned is that such an attitude can be inconsiderate of the people *doing* the job. In order to 'live amicably with others', I must be considerate of others *and* the situation in which we are living and working. There are times, and there are times! Salvation comes through the nature of our relationships, not through the number of prayers I recite nor the religious rituals in which I participate. Setting a good example for others means that my actions come from an authentic place and so they 'shine'. In this case, setting a good example is about being a disciple of Jesus, rather than 'look at me'!

7 August

It is in pardoning that we are pardoned. (St Francis of Assisi)

If I have been wronged then I can clutch my rightness so tightly that I end up using it as a weapon – and not just on 'the offender'. That weapon also harms me. When I pardon someone, my humanity grows. When I pardon someone, the rules and regulations that I also clutched tightly begin to fall away. When I pardon someone, both my heart and my compassion grow. When my compassion grows, I can develop more authentic relationships. When my compassion grows, I can pardon myself for the myriad peccadilloes that I assign as black marks against myself – and realise that they are of little lasting importance.

8 August

To go to the poor is a need of my soul. (Helene de Chappotin)

If we have empathy or compassion, our heartstrings can be tugged when we see the plight of others. What Helene is describing is a much greater sense of purpose but also connection. It is easy to have a patronising attitude towards the poor – to see myself as 'more' or 'greater'. 'Going to the poor' in Helene's mind is more about how she could help and the gifts she might receive. By going to the poor in this way, I see another member of the body of Christ in need. Working with the poor is a wonderful way of being grounded – seeing what truly matters in life without all the 'stuff'. And what truly matters is relationships.

9 August

The very core of the Franciscan spirit is the desire to imitate Jesus Christ in everything, as closely as our human nature will permit. (The Franciscans: Love at Work by Boniface Hanley OFM [Salvator Fink, ©1962 St Anthony's Guild] p. 50)

St Francis has long been an attractive figure due to his simplicity, poverty and connection with nature. Yet all Francis of Assisi strove for was to be like Jesus. He took the words of the Gospel to heart and lived them to the best of his ability. Francis' desire to be like Jesus was 'crowned' when he received the stigmata. Our human nature means that we are all different but if we open ourselves to be shaped by God to be like Christ, good things will happen in each of us: more compassion, less attachment to 'stuff', richer relationships. The 'death' of the ego is the painful part and means that this is a 'path less travelled'.

10 August

We carry out our vocation in the Franciscan way by living the Gospel in the midst of the world following Christ, the humble and poor man simply, peacefully and with joy. (Helene de Chappotin)

Another engaging factor in the Franciscan way is that it is connected to and lived in the everyday world. This is where people and their needs are. This is another area in which Franciscans follow Christ – by being with people. Our church and our world would be a different place if we all lived simply, peacefully and with joy. This idea is so attractive that it is wise to live this way as best I can – working on what prevents me from doing so. Maybe ego?

11 August   St Clare

The kingdom of heaven is promised and given by the Lord only to the poor (Matthew 5:3) for whoever loves temporal things loses the fruits of love. (First letter of St Clare to Agnes of Prague)

Outliving St Francis by twenty-five years, Clare did extraordinary work of her own but also ensured the Franciscan charism continued to burn brightly. The kingdom of heaven comes through justice and right relationships i.e. a focus on people. If my focus is on *things*, then I lose sight of people, so I cannot be in right relationship. If my focus is on things, then I am less concerned about people which is needed for justice.

12 August

Strange
The dark places
We can put ourselves
When the sun is shining.
Fears
Anxiety
Can swallow us.
Then God's grace
Can lift the scales
From our eyes
So we can see
And feel
The light and love
To which we are all called

13 August

*You should make an effort to be so sincere in what
you say that you will earn the reputation of being
entirely truthful, a person whose word can be counted
on, and a person people can rely on. Nothing is more
honourable for you than the sincerity and fidelity you
show in keeping your promises, just as nothing makes
you more worthy of contempt than breaking your
word. (John Baptist De La Salle)*

You have probably heard someone described as 'all talk'.
While we *all* make mistakes, such a person has significant
and repeated gaps between what they say and what they
do. After a while, what such a person says is 'discounted'
with a comment like 'we'll see'. It is through keeping my
word that I become trustworthy. Trust is built over time.
It is only through trust that relationships have a firm
basis. Trust can be eroded more quickly. Broken trust is
acid for relationships. While being forgiving of my own
mistakes and those of others, may I be known for my
integrity.

14 August

*It is chiefly in your actions that your faith should
shine forth. (John Baptist De La Salle)*

It is easy to 'talk a good game'. In the end, we are known
by what we do and thus the phrase: 'actions speak louder
than words'. Faith should lead to action – it is meant
to be lived. This is part of the genius of John's Gospel:

the verb 'to believe' is used 114 times but not the noun 'faith'. Or put differently – faith is a verb. Like Jesus, we need to act in love with and for those around us. As a disciple of Jesus, my loving actions reveal my faith that each person is made in the image of God and deserving of dignity and respect. As a disciple of Jesus, my loving actions build community and bring God's reign closer.

15 August   Feast of the Assumption

I believe that I have taken from Mary the compassion of all souls. I love them all so much. (Helene de Chappotin)

We have the Scriptures and tradition to teach us about Mary. These faith documents promote her as a disciple of Jesus and a person of faith. We understand that she must have had a deep faith to enable her to do as she did. Emboldened by Mary's example, Helene is taking a contemplative approach – seeing the unity of humanity, our connectedness at a deep level. God who is love connects us all. It is with Love that we can have compassion for everyone. This self-sacrificing love helps us to attend to someone's need – grasping in some way, small or large, what unites us all.

16 August

It can be said that you make your real self known by the sort of language you use. (John Baptist De La Salle)

I can think of times when the language and tone that others have used has made me feel crushed. I also cringe when I think of times when my language and tone crushed others – whether I was lashing out or asserting my ego. I'd like to think I've grown as an individual and speak in a way that shows love and care towards everyone in my life as I try to live as a disciple of Jesus. My language also includes humour. My faith is too important to me to not include my whole self. There is no doubt that humour done well can build relationships.

17 August

The Lord made himself poor for us in this world. (St Francis of Assisi)

Jesus made himself poor to show us the way: don't follow the crowd! Don't be swayed by ego and appearances and 'stuff' – the very things that have dominated society for centuries (if not millennia!). Like God, we need to ignore appearances and look at the heart (1 Samuel 16:7). Do I act out of love for others? Am I motivated by compassion and empathy? Is service my focus over status? Do I recognise and foster the good in others? Do I foster relationships?

18 August

Hope doesn't want
To die
But it can seem
Fragile
When fear of a return
To a place of pain
Grips
What seemed clear
Is now clouded.

Be still
Breathe
Trust
In your resources
And the love
From family and friends
That buoys.

Hope is not dead.

19 August

Love at all times, act at all times. This is the secret of
the heart that has understood the love of God. (Helene
de Chappotin)

Many things in life come down to the importance of balance. There are those who wish to distil life to giving intellectual assent to a number of precepts. But what I believe must come to life in my actions. I am commanded to 'love one another' (John 13:34) and this must occur in the concrete reality of my life. The other important point is that the love of God is constant, does not turn off and then on. If I understand that fact, I must love and act constantly. Not just when I feel like it. And not just toward those that seem 'worthy' to me.

20 August

The greatest designs of God upon a soul are only
achieved through opposition. Exterior and interior
trials invigorate the soul. (John Baptist De La Salle)

Our scriptures speak of being 'tested' or 'tried'. There are few of us now whose lives are on the line due to our faith. But the internal opposition of which De La Salle speaks can take the form of our compulsions or addictions. Overcoming them leads to greater self-knowledge and compassion. External opposition has forced me to reflect, to pray, to grope in the darkness, to seek support from those around me and to generally take stock. Neither internal nor external opposition is pleasant but I can increase my compassion as well as gain a greater understanding of my capabilities.

21 August

For God so loved the world that he gave his only Son,
so that everyone who believes in him may not perish
but may have eternal life. (John 3:16)

Jesus is a gift to humanity. Jesus shows us a living and loving that makes us whole if we follow it. Which is why this Gospel has the verb 'believe' – we are meant to live our faith. It makes me whole because it takes me away from my selfish concerns and helps me to build right relationships. This helps to bring God's reign closer. It is also helpful if I spend time reflecting upon God's love for me – especially if my fog of emotions has inclined me to not feel very loveable. My salvation begins in this life. When I am connected with others in right relationships I feel alive rather than a certain 'deadness' from being disconnected.

22 *August*

When we are in a ministry we must add zeal to
action, or else all we do will have but little result.
(John Baptist De La Salle)

First, a ministry is about being of service to others.
Thus it is not merely about actions or 'getting the job
done'. Being of service to others means that I need to
engage with them. This is where zeal comes in. The
person who acts with passion engages others. This is true
in every walk of life – teaching, performing or whatever.
When I act with passion, I draw people in – others want
to know what I'm doing and be part of it. If I minister
with zeal, I go from being efficient to being effective.

23 *August*

He would call creatures, no matter how small, by
the name of 'brother' or 'sister' because he knew they
shared with him the same beginning. (St Bonaventure,
writing of St Francis)

Francis' idea that all life is connected and equivalent,
through the use of 'brother' and 'sister', is *still* a very
radical idea. Wonderfully, science is providing more
and more evidence for this view of creation, past
ecological ideas of the connectedness of living things.
Seeing our connection with creation supports a view of
stewardship (looking after creation 'in trust' for others)
rather than dominion. There is a lot in a word! Seeing
our connection with creation is also a recognition of the

benefits to me, e.g. shade and fresh air from a tree, as
well as psychological and aesthetic benefits.

24 August

Your bounty paints
The whole sky
In another morning
Feast for the eyes
And soul.
I want to stay in the moment
And savour
This delight.

Those
Around me
Seem oblivious.

The moment passes
And I am grateful again
For your grace.
I cannot know others' workings
Yet I wonder:
How are they fed?

25 August

Almighty, most holy most high and supreme God, all good, supreme good, totally good, you who alone are good, may we give back to you all praise, all glory, all grace, all honour, all blessing, and all good. (St Francis of Assisi)

St Francis believed that the whole world is good which is supported by the creation stories in Genesis. Thus everything and everyone in the world is 'good' – and we have God to thank for that. This is a powerful corrective to human egotistical delusions of *our* influence! Truly understanding that God is God allows me to be more free – it *doesn't* depend upon me. This understanding encourages gratitude for all that I am and all that I have. Living in this open-handed way leads to peace.

26 August

Look on everything with the eyes of faith. You must never fail to do this, no matter what the reason. Viewing things with the eyes of faith will earn for you in one day more good, more interior application, closer union with God, and greater vigilance over yourself than a month of those penances and austerities to which you are attracted. Believe me, you will see its effect, though perhaps for the present you will not understand it. (John Baptist De La Salle)

The 'eyes of faith' means that I view the people and situations in my day as opportunities for God's action and guidance in the world. While all our language about God falls short, the eyes of faith means that God's loving action is at work bringing all of creation, including you and me, to fullness. Every person with whom I interact is an opportunity for my growth and/or theirs. I might realise my need for greater compassion or less self-absorption. I might recognise the giftedness of another. I might grasp some of the intricacies of the connectedness of nature. Glimpsing God's work in the world is both comfort and inspiration.

27 August

Faith is the way by which God wishes to lead you to himself and by following this way you will please him most. Is it not enough for you to know God alone? Surely this is of more value than all the other knowledge of the most learned men. (John Baptist De La Salle)

If my focus is knowing God, that is both outward and inward looking. It is looking out as I will focus on fostering right relationships. With those around me – who are also made in the image of God. It is looking out as I will focus on doing what I can to foster justice. It is looking in as I will work on anything in me that prevents me from being my best self and loving others. This leads to my wholeness and holiness. Whereas my ego will work to control me with a focus on what I know and what I can do. A dead end in comparison.

28 August

We are called to love. (Helene de Chappotin)

We believe that we are made in the image and likeness of God. We also believe that God is triune. Thus, we are acting most like the image of God when we give ourselves freely in love to others. My experience is that I am most happy, most content when I behave in this way. Yet, I and others only love in a sparing way. I love like there is a limit. I love in a way that protects me. Helene reminds us that 'we are *called* to love'. Loving is our mission as disciples of Jesus. But there are no conditions and that is scary. Creator God, may I love in such a way that I am a person of integrity.

29 August

I am not speaking metaphorically when I say that it is throughout the length and breadth and depth of the world in movement that humanity can attain the experience and vision of their God. (Teilhard de Chardin Le Milieu Divin, Collins Fontana Books, 1967, p. 36)

Despite the example of St Francis and others down through the centuries, we have taken an anthropocentric view of salvation. Yes, God made everything, but such a view sees that humans are all that *really* matter. Attracting his own share of criticism, Teilhard de Chardin's grand vision of God present in *everything* is closer to describing the scale on which an infinite God works. For too long we have reserved revelation to the scriptures whereas God works on a much broader canvas. Humans have appreciated beauty but not always as of divine origin. Whether we 'like' it or not, whether we can see it or not, God is everywhere. May our eyes be open!

30 August

Apply yourself to interior prayer and try to do all your actions in a prayerful spirit. (John Baptist De La Salle)

Interior prayer is similar to contemplation. It requires practice to do and sustain. In so doing, I acquire a sense of peace, of being centred. All that doesn't matter is shut out or drops away. I allow myself to rest in God's loving gaze. Yet my desire to be 'busy' or 'productive' means that I must dedicate myself to contemplation. I might also avoid contemplation because of self-judgment, feeling unworthy. I must remind myself that God loves me *as I am* – unconditional love. With a contemplative basis, I allow God to direct me and my thoughts and actions. Thus I am more likely to act with integrity.

31 August

We need grace constantly to help us perform our actions properly, to resist the temptations that assail us, and to keep us on the right path. (John Baptist De La Salle)

I can't do things on my own and stay on the right path. This becomes apparent to many people as they live their lives. Grace is God's free gift – which is another way of describing all of creation. In the sense of this quote, it is referring to God's help to stay on course, which relies on a prayerful, contemplative attitude, remaining open to God's guidance in my discernment. This is based in an attitude that I don't have all of the answers, that I am flawed. Once I accept that fact *and* wish to remain true to my faith, I will be open to God's grace and willingly accept it.

SEPTEMBER

1 September

Consider the lilies of the field, how they grow; they
neither toil nor spin, yet I tell you, even Solomon
in all his glory was not clothed like one of these.
(Matthew 6:28-29)

Spring is more about a feeling than a date. There is more sunshine as days get longer which is good for the soul. There is the joy at emerging from the cold and dark of winter. There is also the joy at the abundance of life on show in plants and animals. All this positive affect can encourage us to have a positive attitude about a whole range of matters: work, life, study, relationships. After the introspection and reflection of winter, spring is a time to enact plans and make changes. May you savour all that spring has to offer as well as grasp the opportunities that it presents.

2 September

Do not have any anxiety about the future. Leave
everything in God's hands for he will take care of you.
As for myself, I do not like to make the first move
in any endeavour. I leave it to Divine Providence to
make the first move and then I am satisfied. (John
Baptist De La Salle)

My ego can trick me into thinking that my actions are the instigator for God's will. To truly be doing God's will I need to have a prayerful, contemplative attitude. Without rushing, I will be guided. But my ego rails against this: 'what about me?' The answer is that it is not about me. I am God's heart and hands and feet. God will guide me as God needs to. One cause of anxiety is my thwarted need for control. As has been said – let go and let God. But I think that is easier said than done!

3 September

When we pray, we address God more with the heart than the lips. (John Baptist De La Salle)

We know the importance of prayer for Christians. It is easy to think that prayer is about saying or reciting certain words. What De La Salle reminds us, since prayer is about fostering our relationship with God, is that prayer *should* be about the heart. If I want to be in relationship with God, then my heart should be drawn to God. My heart should also be open to what I might receive. If my heart is 'in the right place' then the words I say matter less. I must take time to rest in God's loving gaze. Then God's love for me can flow into my words and actions.

4 September

Fathers, do not provoke your children to anger, but
bring them up in the discipline and instruction of the
Lord. (Ephesians 6:4)

Putting the 'greeting card' images to one side, Father's Day does not always evoke positive emotions. Both for father and children, it can raise the pain of absence or strained relationships. Those who can should celebrate this day marking close family ties. For others, it is an opportunity to focus on compassion. May I remember the humanity of my daughter, my father, my son and remember my own mistakes and shortcomings. Maybe I have tried, unsuccessfully, to be reconciled. Maybe I have done a lot and don't feel that is being reciprocated. I never lose when I love. It might hurt but these are the growth pains as I more fully resemble my true self – lovingly fashioned by God.

5 September

You may be sure that you will not make progress in
the way of love except insofar as you are faithful not
to harden your heart to the inspirations of grace.
(John Baptist De La Salle)

The way of love is being a disciple of Jesus. The way of love is loving as God does – loving everyone without reserve. I know my faults – I know I need God's help to love and live this way. This is where the 'inspirations of grace' come in. If I am open, God will guide me where I need to be; the people in my life who will help me and whom I will help. But the way of love unravels when I try to go it alone, imposing my will. The way of love is God's way – my ego has to step aside. If I am open, grace has a steady drumbeat for me to follow.

6 September

Smiling
Laughing young people
Under an azure sky
Savouring their release from 'captivity'

We are filled with the sights and smells of spring.
Despite the wind
A camaraderie
Is shared
Goodness flows
Happiness is glimpsed

May we keep our focus
On the good
Remembering that joy
Is the infallible sign of
The presence of God

7 September

The more humble you are, the more graces you will receive. (John Baptist De La Salle)

Humility can be misunderstood. Humility is an acceptance of my giftedness without the need to tell all and sundry about it. While there may be cultural factors, it is only the insecure or the egotistical (is there a difference?) that need to strongly promote themselves. If I am humble, my acceptance of my giftedness means that I am welcoming of others and their gifts and talents. This attitude makes relationships easier – with all the benefits or graces that entails. Such connections bring joy, love and peace – graces indeed.

8 September

I have asked that the reign of true power, of love, will spread from me to many others. (Helene de Chappotin)

This is not ego, rather its opposite. Openly or by stealth, ego is about taking. Love is about giving and connecting. As a leader, Helene's example mattered. Rather than set up some cult of ego, she inspired a group of women to be true to the Gospel and the Franciscan ideals of poverty. Her wish was granted in that there are ministries all over the world caring for those in need, such as a variety of pastoral works including babies born with AIDS and women ensnared by human trafficking. Love from women inspired by Helene, delicately and generously applied, helps in these and similar situations to guide those in their care towards wholeness.

9 *September*

Be satisfied with what you can do, since God is
satisfied... be convinced that with divine help you can
do more than you imagine. (John Baptist De La Salle)

I need to understand my place in the scheme of things. I do my part but it does *not* all depend upon me. My ego can feel me into thinking differently. Yet, each person plays their part in community. Am I using and making the most of my gifts? Am I helping others to make the most of their gifts? Another key is to remember that we are each doing God's work. If I remember that and am turned outward in love to others, great things happen. I pray that is something you already *know.*

10 *September*

Look upon humility as the foundation of all the
other moral virtues, without which there can be no
true piety. Piety, without humility, is usually mere
hypocrisy or an illusion. (John Baptist De La Salle)

Humility is a sense both of my abilities and my limitations. Humility opens me toward others – both what I can give and what I need. I need to have a sense of my limitations to know how much I need God and others. If I am trying to follow God, follow Jesus, my spiritual practices should make me thirst for God and become more aware of my need to work on my shortcomings so that I can relate better to others. My spiritual practices should encourage me to be God's heart and hands in the world. Without humility, I can start to judge – which is not my job and acid for relationships.

11 *September*

Be moderate in your conduct and observe discretion in
your words. (John Baptist De La Salle)

I am still working on this! I'm fairly confident that my discretion has improved over the years. My ego has flaunted my 'knowledge' of something or other – which has been unhelpful. I have been described as having a 'peaceful presence' but I also know that my conduct might also be described as 'flamboyant'. In the end, we each need to own and embrace who we are. The key is to remember we live in community and I need to ensure my behaviour and words build others up – not pull them down.

12 September

One of our chief duties should be to learn to speak of God and to speak well of him. (John Baptist De La Salle)

Learning a language requires persistence. It is no different if we are to be 'real' about our faith. In order to provide an example to others, I must be able to be clear about my own faith to then be able to speak about it. My experience is that this is something that comes with time. Thus the wisdom in 'learning to speak of God'. There is also the impediment of our culture that is not comfortable with God language. It is easy to sound unctuous, separated from reality or as a cover for the darkness or compulsions in my heart. Our faith is in a God who loves each of us into wholeness. May we also walk the talk.

13 September

Trees buffeted by the breeze
Clothes spin around on the line
Vines and bushes and grass
Verdant
In the midst of spring

Sitting outside
Absorbing this tableau
I am struck
By the blue backdrop
The sky
With no clouds
Only brilliant sunshine
So vast
As to draw everything
Into itself

14 September

*If I say, 'I will not mention him or speak any more
in his name', then within me there is something like
a burning fire shut up in my bones; I am weary with
holding it in, and I cannot. (Jeremiah 20:9)*

My faith helps me to make sense of myself, my
relationships and the world around me. This is
something that has deepened and strengthened over
the years such that it is 'in my bones'. Part of my life's
journey is to learn to be true to who I am. That entails

using the gifts that I have been given. As much as I do that, all is well. The 'fire within me' is being used as it should. Like Jeremiah, I may not always be popular but it is more important to be true to myself. Am I using all of my gifts? Am I helping others to name and use their gifts?

15 September

Then God said, 'Come no closer! Remove the sandals from your feet, for the place on which you are standing is holy ground'. (Exodus 3:5)

This holy ground requires human interaction – no shoes – but contact of skin with ground. Is this standing before God as we were created? I'm not sure that the concept of 'holy ground' is very prevalent today, but I'm sure that people have times, places or people that are sacred to them. 'Holy ground' could be a special relationship – such as with my wife. We love, foster and support each other to become whole. 'Holy ground' could be a sunrise, sunset or when a special flower is in bloom. 'Holy ground' could be a birthday celebration or a Christmas gathering. 'Holy ground' is where we encounter God in the reality of our lives. What's your holy ground?

16 September

So God created humankind in his image, in the image
of God he created them; male and female he created
them. (Genesis 1:27)

So much flows from this passage. We are each creations of God – made good and all that we are comes from God. We are made in God's image – each of us. Thus I should respect myself and every person with whom I deal as they, too, are made in God's image. Since we believe God is triune and in a relationship of love within Godself, having loving relationships is another way that we act in God's image. Another point from this passage is that male and female are made in God's image – no one greater or lesser, just different. Learning to live in complementarity is one of life's joys!

17 September

Take a short recreation every day so that you may
afterwards resume your duties with greater affection
and application. Look upon this relaxation as similar
to that which our Lord sometimes accorded his
disciples. (John Baptist De La Salle)

It is important that I give myself a break – as well as those around me. I need to factor in time every day to appreciate life – to just be. It could be through music or time in nature – whatever will charge my batteries. If I focus solely on work, I am likely to lose my 'reason why' or my work will become unsatisfying. If I take time out, I am more likely to be positive, more likely to be 'good news' to those around me. Similarly, whether it is through a joke or some other means that I give others a break, it shares an awareness of our important human need for recreation so that my doing has more heart and more impact.

18 September

Then the Lord God said, 'See, the man has become like one of us, knowing good and evil; and now, he might reach out his hand and take also from the tree of life, and eat, and live forever'. (Genesis 3:22)

Note that the Lord God uses the plural 'like one of us'. Long before any Trinitarian theology, we are left to speculate. Another point is that the human has gained the *divine* power of knowing good and evil. If we explore history, we can find plenty of examples when the good was ignored, mostly for the sake of money and power. It is also interesting to note the Jewish wisdom tradition, the Kabbalah, sees the creation story more as humans growing into themselves, rather like the teenage years. May we each act on our knowledge of good and evil.

19 September

St Francis shows us just how inseparable the bond is between concern for nature, justice for the poor, commitment to society, and interior peace. (Pope Francis, Laudato Sí, 10)

The coherence being referred to is wrapped up in our understanding of God. If we believe God is in everything and everyone, then it makes perfect sense that nature, justice for the poor and commitment to society are all connected – as we saw in the life of St Francis. And as we have spoken, prayer and contemplation are vital to discern God's plan for me. This will give interior peace rather than ego-driven restlessness. Consider: do I see God in everything and everyone? Do I glimpse the connectedness? Do I grasp the importance of justice *and* right relationships?

20 September

What is more, Saint Francis, faithful to Scripture, invites us to see nature as a magnificent book in which God speaks to us and grants us a glimpse of his infinite beauty and goodness. (Pope Francis, Laudato Sí, *12)*

It is a Franciscan saying that the book of nature and the book of scripture have the same author, God. It is a refrain in Genesis that 'God saw all that he had made and it was good'. Humans have their perspective and may not always see the goodness of certain aspects of creation. Yet the more study that has been done, the more complex the interactions in nature prove to be – and there is beauty in those interactions along with the appearance. God is speaking to us to have a broader perspective than just our own, if something has a purpose other than human use; to be stewards rather than dominators as we hold the beauty in trust for future generations. Finally, to let the beauty and goodness speak to us and make us whole.

21 September

Another day begins
And I get ready
Physically
And mentally
Planning
Checking.
It's so easy for me
To get caught up.

I walk out the door and am dazzled
By the reds and oranges,
Apricot, blue and grey
Of the sunrise
And I remember
What truly matters.
You are always
With me

22 *September*

We discover togetherness in community, and that
difference is not a threat but a treasure. (Jean Vanier)

We are each saved in and by community. I can confront my mistakes and shortcomings when I hurt those I care for. In so doing, I become more truly myself. Community is also a place to belong that is very important for the growth of each of us. I suspect that it is because of my reptilian brain that I see those not like me as a threat. While that may have been true in the distant past, I have so much I can learn from someone who is different to me. Each culture lives life differently – and there is a richness in each. Momentarily stepping outside of my own way of living life can hold up a mirror to it – and I may glimpse a better, more fully human way to live my life. The study of other languages and cultures can open such a window. Our shared humanity is so much greater than any seeming differences. Unity in diversity *is* the body of Christ.

23 *September*

Francis asked that part of the friary garden always
be left untouched, so that wild flowers and herbs
could grow there, and those who saw them could raise
their minds to God, the Creator of such beauty. (Pope
Francis, Laudato Sí, *12)*

As humans we have a drive for order that sidelines the wild, untamed. Yet this completely natural state is as

God intended. The natural state could have a variety of ecological purposes as well as a source of wonder and beauty for we humans – and thus an opportunity to see and value God's creation. Do I allow the wild space in my life? Do I praise God in God's creation? Is God the centre of my world?

24 September

*The sacrifice acceptable to God is a broken spirit;
a broken and contrite heart, O God, you will not
despise. (Psalm 51:17)*

It is easy to think that I need to be 'good enough' for God. The reality is that I am already good enough, with my flaws. The only uncertainty is the length of time between my mistakes! Embracing my flawed nature is the key to my salvation – I need to be saved from myself. If I get too caught up in ego, I can become blinded to my mistakes. Owning my flawed nature means that I 'approach' God appropriately. 'A broken and contrite heart' means that I do not place myself above others. 'A broken and contrite heart' makes it more likely that I will glimpse God in others as I am in relationship with them. I will realise my need – and it will be met by the God who loved me into life.

25 September

Nothing disposes us better to receive the Holy Spirit than prayer. (John Baptist De La Salle)

Prayer is our communication guide with God. One way of understanding the Holy Spirit is God's love at work in the world. Of course, the two go together! As disciples of Jesus, we need the Holy Spirit to guide us so that we are doing God's work and *not* our own. Similar to another quote, prayer and contemplation open me to be aware of God's influence in my life. Prayer allows me to grasp and then co-operate with the Holy Spirit at work in my life.

26 September

Simon Peter answered him, 'Lord, to whom can we go? You have the words of eternal life'. (John 6:68)

A variety of events can shake my faith: death of a loved one, a seemingly intractable problem, a crime by a prominent church member. I may wrestle with the situation for some time. Eventually, I am faced with Peter's question: to whom can I go? It can come down to patience – to wait until a solution emerges despite my need to 'progress'. Maybe I need to trust – that God has my interests at heart, despite my need for control. These or other limits on my faith, my believing in Jesus, hold me back from the life to the full to which I am called. So, I just need to get over myself!

27 September

Many of the poor live in areas particularly affected by phenomena related to warming, and their means of subsistence are largely dependent on natural reserves and eco- systemic services such as agriculture, fishing and forestry. (Pope Francis, Laudato Sí, *25)*

There is a big picture. There are those who make significant amounts of money from 'business as usual'. They are driven by profit. Business as usual has led us to a variety of pressures on ecological systems. Some of this has been documented by the Intergovernmental Panel on Climate Change (www.ipcc.ch). Those who are doing well currently discredit or sideline the views of those looking for change. What some, including Pope Francis, have grasped is that this is not just an ecological problem but it is a justice issue as well, including those who are subsistence farmers. If I value God's creation, then I must value all of it, not just the parts I like or want. May I see that God is calling me to more.

28 September

Waves surge and crash
Their elemental force
throbbing

Thick mist broods
over leaden waters
until a crack of blue sky
and the sun sneaks through

Magnificent rocky cliffs
jut out of the water
now blue
from the sun and sky

And out to sea
still broods
the massive bank of fog
whose tendrils occasionally
lick the shore

29 September

Because of us, thousands of species will no longer give
glory to God by their very existence, nor convey their
message to us. We have no such right. (Pope Francis,
Laudato Sí, 33)

If I see nature as something over which humans have
dominion, then I need to change the way I think.

Humans are *part* of God's creation not *apart* from. Other species do not revolve around humanity and their worth is *not* measured by their worth to humanity. The extraordinary complexity in nature is part of God's design. The more species that are lost, it is like taking strands from a tapestry – the whole is both frayed and lacking in richness and beauty. I have a responsibility to examine my actions in order to minimise the impact on species through my use of resources. This is a practical way I care for God's creation.

30 September

You are held to the love of prayer in order to attract the power needed for your own holiness as well as that of others. (John Baptist De La Salle)

Being holy only makes sense when I am connected to God. If I am not connected to God, why be holy? Thus being holy is not something I do on my own but because of my connection with God. Prayer and contemplation is the way to foster my relationship with God. So prayer and contemplation help me to be holy; it is not something I do by or for myself. Being whole and holy means that I am turned toward others. This is the attitude that will help my wholeness and holiness, and that of others.

OCTOBER

1 October

'Praised be'
Sang our spiritual guide
Directing our gaze
Towards the incandescent echoes
Of infinite Love
All around us
Every day.

Wonders and delights
Such as
The verdant glow of trees
The flower's delicate aroma
Another spectacular sunrise
Or sunset
The windswept breakers roll in to the beach
A baby's infectious giggle
Family, friends, work colleagues
With which we have been gifted
All guiding us
Towards the source of all good.

In our headlong rush
Through our days
We can be blind to these joys.
Rather let us embrace
The 'wow' of the child
Which is why we need to be childlike
To enter and embrace God's reign

2 October

It may well disturb us to learn of the extinction of mammals or birds, since they are more visible. But the good functioning of ecosystems also requires fungi, algae, worms, insects, reptiles and an innumerable variety of microorganisms. (Pope Francis, Laudato Sí, 34)

'I believe in one God... creator of all things, seen and unseen....'. So goes the Nicene Creed, summary of Christian faith for 1700 years. Yet, humans are largely focussed on what can be seen. When species loss is spoken of, there is a focus on mammals and birds. The grand design placed by God in creation is much more complex, including the recycling and reuse of nutrients like nitrogen, carbon and a vast array of other compounds that are vital for all life. And as much as humans deplete the ecosystem, they can also put too much in – too much in the way of nitrogen compounds in waterways leads to algal blooms which can choke and kill water life as part of a process called eutrophication. Such thoughtless behaviour is disrespectful to God as creator.

3 October

I am the bread of life. (John 6:48)

Another of the 'I am' sayings refers to it being part of God's nature to nourish humanity so that we are 'fed'. But not in a short term way. Rather, following Jesus, living as Jesus did will give me life. It is life-giving to live in right relationship with those around me, respecting each person as an image of God worthy of respect, dignity and compassion. It is life giving to read the scriptures as well as foster a relationship with God through prayer and contemplation. It is also life-giving to work for justice, mindful of those on the margins of life and how their dignity and respect are being compromised.

4 October   St Francis

Where does it begin?
Community puts down roots
In the hearts of each
Its leaves and branches
Spring forth
In word and deed
Animated
By the richly poor man
From Assisi

Based in faith
Of the richly poor man
From Nazareth

From the young
And the less so
Comes
The encouraging word
Plenty of smiling 'hellos'
Support in time of need
Praise for effort
Supportive challenge
Loving correction
Laughs and jokes
Thought-provoking questions
Reflection and prayer

Such caring expressions
Bind us together
And so we become what we believe
God *is* love

5 October

In the beginning was the Word, and the Word was
with God, and the Word was God. (John 1:1)

A word exists to be spoken, to be heard and acted upon.
So John establishes that the Word existed before time
in and with God and was *part* of creation, since 'in the
beginning' are the same words as Genesis 1:1. The Word
is Jesus Christ and John leaves us under no illusion as
to the divinity of the Word. It is little wonder that this
Gospel helps form the basis of Trinitarian theology.
Some questions to ponder are: Am I hearing God's
word? Do I make space in my life to hear God's word?
Am I acting upon God's word in my life?

6 October

A sober look at our world shows that the degree of
human intervention, often in the service of business
interests and consumerism, is actually making our
earth less rich and beautiful, ever more limited and
grey, even as technological advances and consumer
goods continue to abound limitlessly. (Pope Francis,
Laudato Sí, 34)

Humans can think they know what they're doing and
that they control things. Complex ecosystems respond
in ways that humans do not always foresee. Driven by
a profit motive can make the focus too narrow: 'so long
as I am fine'. This has played out in many ways over
the last 200 years, such that it is not only Pope Francis

who has said that activity has made 'our earth less rich and beautiful, ever more limited and grey'. Those in developed countries 'have' so much more – but at what cost? 'For what will it profit someone to gain the whole world and yet lose their life?' (Mark 8:36)

7 October

Prayer also gives us special strength to endure patiently everything we find most difficult. (John Baptist De La Salle)

Life's difficulties can be caused by my rough edges rubbing up against another person's rough edges. Such rough edges can be caused by ego, obsession or a myriad of other failings. Prayer can help give me patience – with myself and others. Sometimes the difficulties I face are external such as the illness of a loved one. Prayer might nudge me toward patience and acceptance of the situation. As much as situations are difficult, this is life. As the poet Kahlil Gibran said, 'Our cups must be hollowed by sorrow so that they can be filled to the brim with joy'.

8 October

Love is to be celebrated
Always and everywhere
When we diminish love
We diminish our humanity
When we promote love
We promote human unity
And fan the divine spark into flame

Love
Brings us together
Emphasising the good in each other
Surmounting the challenges
That society and others
Might put in the way

True love is a gift
Not just for the couple
But for all they meet.
The circle of love
Expands to be inclusive
As seen in the newly married Richard and Werner
Warmth, hospitality and gentle humour

As St Paul said,
'There are many gifts...
... and the greatest of these is love'.

9 October

These are signs that the growth of the past two centuries has not always led to an integral development and an improvement in the quality of life. (Pope Francis, Laudato Sí, 46)

As much as humans can use God's creation wisely, these resources are for everyone – not for some. Certainly, they are not to benefit a small number of people astronomically more than others. Nor should the resources be used as a means of enslaving others or making them feel less. The consumer culture of developed countries is predicated on continual growth. While the resources of God's creation are bountiful, they are not limitless. As big as Earth is, it is finite. A refrain from those who participate in immersion programs to developing countries: 'they have so little and yet they are so happy'. Makes you think!

10 October

Today's media do enable us to communicate and to share our knowledge and affections. Yet at times they also shield us from direct contact with the pain, the fears and the joys of others and the complexity of their personal experiences. (Pope Francis, Laudato Sí, 47)

Whether through fact or fiction, the media through which we receive information has been the subject of cautionary tales. George Orwell's *1984* is an example. Factual reporting of events that do not suit political ends is called 'fake news'. It is easy for problems to be 'over there' or 'someone else's' – each person's life does present its own challenges. Yet, we are saved by and for community. We are each made in the image of God and so we can learn so much from others – about compassion, about grace, about dignity. If we hold the lives of others at arm's length, we cannot be touched by them.

11 October

And the Word became flesh and lived among us, and we have seen his glory, the glory as of a father's only son, full of grace and truth. (John 1:14)

In this passage, John is also keen to establish that Jesus was fully human – 'he lived among us'. The words also establish the Incarnation. The prologue also establishes the eyewitness backing of this account: 'we have seen his glory'. As Dorothy Lee points out, God's glory is visible in humans. Pondering on this directs us to treat those around us with dignity and respect since God's glory is visible in them. Do I live my faith in the Incarnation? We note the echo of Luke's description of Mary, 'full of grace', and grace comes from God. Time and again, John returns to Jesus and truth. There is divine certainty in Jesus.

12 October

Just as light is necessary in this world, just as we need life in our body to preserve it, and just as a sick person needs medicine to get well, so too prayer is necessary for the soul that serves God. (John Baptist De La Salle)

Our lives can be so busy that we 'don't have time to pray'. If that is the case, my doing will have less meaning, be less effective than if I *make* time to pray. How can I serve God if I am not connected to God in prayer? I can mean well, be well intentioned but my ego is so strong, so immediate that it will get in the way. My ego is very likely to lead me down a blind alley. So prayer and contemplation is necessary to ensure that I am aware of God's promptings in my life, then to follow those promptings rather than my ego. I am much more likely to be doing a good job of serving God.

13 October

Why would I write about addiction? My family has a history of addiction (and recovery), including my father, so it is part of who I am. I also recognise that my obsessive tendencies could take me to addiction but my wife's love has been my anchor. My experience of 12 step programs is that they are real, honest, sane and deeply human with a process and a community that has much to offer. Rooted in early Christianity, I offer the 12 steps to you in some of the following reflections. You might recognise yourself in one or more of the steps and so be drawn closer to the God who loves each of us unconditionally.

First step: We admitted we were powerless over (our addicted 'thing') – that our lives had become unmanageable.

I have made the 12 steps generic because there are so many things that I can become addicted to – other than alcohol and other drugs. I might be addicted to sex or power or any number of other things. To admit I have a problem is indeed the first step to fixing it. We live in a world of agency – I need to be in control. So to admit I am powerless is huge. The first step admits the addiction is running my life and thus limiting me from all that I can be. This is easier said than done as addiction has a way of fooling me: 'I am helping others'; 'I am my best self when I do this'; 'It helps me cope'; 'I'm no different from anyone else'. But then something happens to open my eyes...

14 October

Both everyday experience and scientific research show that the gravest effects of all attacks on the environment are suffered by the poorest. (Pastoral letter of Bolivian Bishops, 2012, quoted in Pope Francis, Laudato Sí, 48)

Issues can be categorised as 'social justice' or 'environmental'. Sometimes people can focus on one or the other. In so doing, we can neglect the connection between the two. The poorest in developing countries might have their subsistence farming prevented by massive pollution or more frequent dramatic weather events e.g. 'super typhoons' in the Philippines. The poorest in developed countries might live/work near polluting industries. Environmental issues most frequently have social effects. The two are connected.

15 October

As I blithely go about
My schedule
And my days
Life is a succession
Of moments
That can swirl
Past me
If I'm not
Paying attention

A glorious vista of turquoise and aqua waters
Framed by leaden skies
Illuminated by the morning sun

Moments of light
Amidst seeming gloom
A wink
A woman lovingly rocking
A baby to sleep
A toddling explorer
Roaming his domain

Then the extraordinary
Ordinary
Ten lorikeets atop the grevillea
The frangipani's first bloom
For this summer

Moments
Easily missed
Small
Great
Graced
To take my breath away
That allow God
To touch my heart

16 October

*Jesus said, 'I ask not only on behalf of these, but also
on behalf of those who will believe in me through
their word, that they may all be one. As you, Father,
are in me and I am in you, may they also be in us, so
that the world may believe that you have sent me'.
(John 17:20-21)*

We who believe in Jesus Christ are joined in faith
– but the human obstacles that have been created
through history! Only a fool would ignore schisms but
a course in Trinitarian theology with other Christian
denominations twenty years ago convinced me that
what unites (implicit in this passage) is *much* greater
than what divides us. What we need to do is to live our
lives based in that unity, rather than place obstacles in
the way of God's plan.

17 October

The Lord says to the prisoners, 'Come out',
*   to those who are in darkness, 'Show yourselves'.*
(Isaiah 49:9)

In today's society, how many people are 'in a prison'? It could be the darkness of constant physical pain. It might be the prison of addiction – where I find my way out only to be drawn back in. It might be the shadow of the struggle with mental health. It might be the pain of difficult or lost relationships. What I must realise is that the situation (whatever it is) is *not* God's punishment on me. Rather, God loves me into life and wants only my wholeness and happiness. And if I can grasp God's love for me, it might be possible for me to push open the cell door...

18 October

His mother said to the servants, 'Do whatever he tells you'. (John 2:5)

There are striking things about this passage. Jesus has just told his mother (Mary is not named in the Gospel of John) that his hour had not yet come but seeing the need at the wedding and knowing Jesus can help, she ignores him. She tells the servants to wait for his instructions. As a parent, Mary 'knows better' than her son. She also has faith in her son, even if he is 'stalling'. The Gospels clearly convey the message of Jesus: the importance of a relationship with God through prayer; the importance of helping those 'on the outer' of society; obeying the spirit rather than the letter of the law; the importance of not judging others and having compassion. Our task is to live up to 'do whatever he tells you'.

19 October

The application to the presence of God by simple attention consists in being before God in a simple interior view of faith that he is present. Remain thus for some time, say ten or fifteen minutes, according to how you feel yourself occupied by and interiorly attracted to it. (John Baptist De La Salle)

De La Salle continues the thread of contemplation begun centuries earlier. Practical man that he was, his instructions are clear but not prescriptive. This shows someone who is aware of the ebb and flow of contemplation. It is an act of faith – God is present with me in contemplation. I rest in God's loving gaze. Beginning or continuing can have its challenges such as carving out time daily. There are always distractions, activities that claim my time. The practice of contemplation brings peace – always a prized commodity.

20 October

These days, they (the excluded) are mentioned in international political and economic discussions, but one often has the impression that their problems are brought up as an after-thought, a question which gets added almost out of duty or in a tangential way, if not treated merely as collateral damage. (Pope Francis,
Laudato Sí, *49)*

'You can't make an omelette without breaking some eggs.' Such a saying stands to reason and experience – except when the 'eggs' are people. Decision-making on a global stage is utilitarian, but with a twist. The 'greatest number' usually reside among the developed countries. Frequently, the issues of real people with little or no voice are sidelined. Franciscans International (franciscansinternational.org) is a voice for the voiceless at the United Nations. I think it will be helpful for all of us to get our facts about a situation from as many places as possible so that we can see the whole picture.

21 October

Second step: Came to believe that a Power greater than ourselves could restore us to sanity.

If my life is unmanageable, then this second step implies that I am lacking in sanity i.e. my behaviour is unreasonable or irrational. And since my life is 'out of control', *I* can't get it back under control, only my higher power can, that I call God. I believe in a higher power through establishing a relationship and feeling supported and maybe even a sense of relief that it *doesn't* all depend upon me when I have so spectacularly screwed things up. Thus slowly through my challenges and missteps I have a growing sense that God is there, loving and caring for me despite my failures.

22 October

I believe in one God,
maker of heaven and earth,
of all things visible and invisible. (Nicene Creed)

Similar to the 10 commandments, the Nicene Creed affirms monotheism. Rather than the many gods in the Greco-Roman world, Christianity affirms one God. This God made everything – what we can see and what we can't see but know is present, like the wind. This is also a direct link to the accounts of creation in Genesis 1-2. Even more than that, I need to live my life *in that belief* of one God. Thus, my sole focus is not on money, nor power, nor prestige, nor possessions, nor any other *thing* that takes my focus away from God and the *relationships* that make me whole.

23 October

You only know as much as you do. (St Francis of Assisi)

One way of understanding what Francis is referring to is the difference between knowledge and wisdom. As someone who has spent my life in education, it is easy to focus on knowledge. Yet it is when knowledge is enacted that it has real power. Languages and the humanities should teach about seeing the world from more than just my perspective – there are so many other valid ways of living life and seeing the world. From this I can learn compassion and empathy. Likewise, my religious beliefs have true power when I live them. Treating each person with dignity and respect since they are made in God's image. Living forgiveness and compassion builds right relationships and means that I live like the image of God that I am.

24 October

Apply yourself often to remember the presence of God. Look upon this practice as your greatest happiness. Your recollection and self-control should be great enough for you to achieve this. (John Baptist De La Salle)

I love being with friends. I'm sure you do too! Easy laughter, shared meals, sometimes holidays. Spending time in that way is precious. Contemplation is time spent with God. While it can be difficult, it gives peace. That which is unimportant drops away. As a human being, this is an opportunity to *be*, not solely focus on *doing*. As helpful as doing can be, it can have a compulsive edge. God loves me, as I am. Sitting with that, allowing it to sink in, also allows my self-judgment to drop away. Resting in love is life-giving; it brings peace, makes me whole.

25 October

Jesus said to them, 'Very truly, I tell you, before Abraham was, I am'. (John 8:58)

Jesus is having a heated argument with 'the Jews'. Since Jesus himself was a Jew, the term 'the Jews' is a term in John's Gospel referring to the Jews who did not believe in Jesus. After much to and fro in this argument, Jesus is looking to end it (or is he just looking to make it more heated?). Using the name for God from Exodus 3, the eternal present, this could be seen as trump card and/or hand grenade. Jesus is not just saying he is more important than Abraham but that he is pre-existent with God. For us, the Christ transcends all barriers and limitations. Don't think you know where God is – God is everywhere including those places we may not expect!

26 October

I had another jolt
Of awareness
As I glimpsed
The orange and red
Of the morning sky
Which blessed
All who had the privilege
Of seeing it

I flash past
The epicentre of this wonder
Then it is gone.
Like the reflections
On the clouds
I am left with echoes

This tableau
Delights my soul
I wasn't sure
Whether to laugh or cry
And it leaves me
Wanting more
So much more

27 October

*Third step: Made a decision to turn our will and our
lives over to the care of God as we understood God.*

A key factor of the 12 steps is fellowship – I am not trying to recover from my addiction by myself. Support from others who are also struggling or have struggled is crucial. Due to addiction, my decision-making hasn't always been sound; my will has got my life in a mess. Through prayer and contemplation, I grow in self-knowledge and I also grow in understanding of God's plan for me i.e. what is best for me. My growing relationship with God encourages me to hand my will over to the God who loves me into wholeness. Depending upon my addiction, by handing my will and life over to God, the only way is up! What do I need to turn my will over to God for today?

28 October

Fourth step: Made a searching and fearless moral inventory of ourselves.

If I resolve to do and be better with God's help, then I need to honestly face what I have done. As an addict, there may be multiple 'train wrecks' but what is the path that took me there? Discerning patterns in my behaviour allows me then to understand why these patterns exist. This step is challenging and it would be easy to dodge it, but how can I progress if I have not been honest with myself? As part of this inventory I can also acknowledge where I've got it right, even if things haven't turned out right OR the good seems small.

29 October

*We have to realise that a true ecological approach
always becomes a social approach; it must integrate
questions of justice in debates on the environment, so
as to hear both the cry of the earth and the cry of the
poor. (Pope Francis, Laudato Sí, 49)*

Having established the connection between questions
of justice and the environment, the key is to be able to
see the points of connection or overlap in any given
situation. When there is a tension, it is easiest to give
way to one pole or the other. This is an occasion when
both must remain in balance. Humans live in the
environment. If the balance is solely towards humans,
the environment will become so badly degraded as to
eventually affect humans (as is the case now?). Whereas
if the balance is towards the environment, then humans
may not be able to carry on their lives. Such a balance
requires good information, wisdom and political will –
as well as God's grace.

30 October

*Do not have any anxiety about the future. Leave
everything in God's hands for he will take care of you.
(John Baptist De La Salle)*

To live by this requires faith. Not to have any anxiety
about the future requires complete trust in God. For
'worry warts' like me, it is easier said than done! I believe
intellectually that God will take care of me – and I have

plenty of examples in my life where God *has* looked after me. Yet, my anxiety will easily overtake me. Clearly, this is an area of growth for me! Time and again I will catch myself worrying – and everything works out fine. I will keep chipping away at this. Maybe you can relate?

31 October

Lost in the fog
Of the emotions
That I've made
For myself
Then I'm jolted
Alert
By another's pain
Borne with grace
And again
By the proud father
Holding his baby
And a third time
By a gentle laugh
With strangers

We have a choice:
Turn outward
And connect with others
Or
Stay in our private hell.

No brainer?

NOVEMBER

1 *November*

He said, 'Lord, I believe'. And he worshipped him.
(John 9:38)

At the conclusion of this masterfully told story of 'sight' and 'blindness', the man born blind has come to full faith in Jesus. The story tracks the man receiving his physical sight and growing in spiritual sight. So it is for most of us. Sometimes my faith in Jesus can be intellectual assent rather than demonstrated in my behaviour. Do I go to those on the margins? Do I act with compassion and forgiveness? Do I foster right relationships? Do I work for justice? It is in my life that I believe in Jesus.

2 *November*

These achievements do not solve global problems, but they do show that men and women are still capable of intervening positively. (Pope Francis, Laudato Sí, *58)*

It is *not* all doom and gloom. There are individuals and groups who have done good work caring for the environment. These are signs of positivity and hope. However, such actions generally address a localised issue. The circumstances of climate change require a co-ordinated systemic response. Such a response is best enacted at a governmental level. The real difficulty at a governmental level is getting past egos, agendas and other petty differences to be able to carve out a solution. Given the state of matters, giving up is not an option – so it's about having the determination to see it through.

While I might feel powerless, am I guided by such matters when I vote?

3 November

> *It frequently happens that what we attempt does not succeed as we had expected, because we undertook it on our own initiative, and because we follow no other rule and no other guide than what our own spirit is able to propose. St Peter told Jesus Christ that he had laboured all night without catching a single fish; the reason for this was that he had acted entirely on his own. (John Baptist De La Salle)*

You may have heard a young child say: 'do it self'. It is the natural way of things for a young child to increase its agency – to prove that it can. However, as an adult who professes to be a disciple of Jesus then it's not about what *I* want to do. If I am wise, I open myself through prayer to be guided by God in my actions. My experience is that if you look for guidance from God you will get it, in spades. I will also find guidance in the scriptures. If I 'go it alone', I'm less likely to be effective. We see again the importance of parking the ego.

4 November

*Fifth step: Admitted to God, to ourselves and to
another human being the exact nature of our wrongs.*

Given its nature, a number of things need to be ready
before I begin this step. It is one matter to set it all out
but it is a huge step to be clear about all of my areas of
improvement. I need to admit all my errors to myself as
well as to God if I am to foster a strong relationship with
God whom I've admitted is my true way forward. This is
significant but to admit to everything I have done wrong,
out loud, to someone else is massive. I need to know I
trust this person implicitly. Maybe I admit my wrongs to
my sponsor or someone else who has travelled my road,
given that this is deeply intimate. As fearful as I may be
beforehand, so long as I have chosen my person well, a
weight will be lifted from me.

5 November

*Sixth step: We're entirely ready to have God remove
all of these defects of character.*

People behave in certain ways that others can judge as
negative because there is kind of a 'pay off' or 'upside'.
I am not so proud of hurting people because of my
addiction or how I behave in that state. Yet, I enjoy feeling
'out of it' or not feeling or forgetting my troubles. The
sixth step is my choice to say 'I'm done with my former
lifestyle and I want to change'. It also acknowledges
that this change only happens through God's free gift

of grace. It is not my work; I cannot change me; only God can do that. I can see that what seemed good is destructive and must be changed. Am I ready to let go of old, fearful behaviours?

6 November

Jesus said to her, 'I am the resurrection and the life'.
(John 11:25)

In the midst of dealing with the death of his friend Lazarus, Jesus' statement is provocative. It jolts those grieving to think in a less linear way – which is difficult to do when I am grieving. For the readers of the Gospel, it is a different matter, yet no less provocative. If I say I believe in Jesus then I need to live that way – seeing the life that living brings. It is also helpful if my understanding of resurrection is broader. The ways that a person grows out of a difficult situation is a form of resurrection. The ways that someone rebuilds their life out of addiction is a form of resurrection. When do I glimpse resurrection?

7 November

*The ultimate destiny of the universe is in the fullness
of God, which has already been attained by the risen
Christ, the measure of the maturity of all things.
(Pope Francis, Laudato Sí, 83)*

Father, Son and Holy Spirit are in a mutual in-dwelling
of love. The Trinity is not just a concept but an expression
of God's love for all creation. This loving connection
gathers up everything. Each thing, animate and
inanimate, is an expression of God's love and a means
by which other parts of creation reach their fullness.
This can occur through working *with* God's plan and
thus creating harmony. How am I contributing to this?

8 November

*Everybody has defects, and we bring them with
us everywhere we go. Consequently, it is only by
overlooking them among ourselves that we can
maintain peace and union even in the most select
societies. This is why St Paul says that charity endures
all things. (John Baptist De La Salle)*

My ego rarely allows me to become aware of my defects.
If one occurs, my ego will say to me 'let's not dwell on
that'. Yet, if I focus on the plank in my own eye rather
than the speck in someone else's eye, I become more
compassionate and less judgmental. I will still be aware
of other's faults – my rough edges rub against your rough
edges so there will be friction – but I am more likely to

move past them. In so doing, we more closely model right relationships and so bring God's reign closer.

9 *November*

Staring at a stand of eucalypts
Rustling leaves in the trees
Other leaves float down
Sporadically
And kind of magically
Sometimes in flurries.
An echidna ambles by.
I feel a pull of energy
From my physical centre
Drawing me in
To be one

10 *November*

Seventh step: Humbly asked God to remove our shortcomings.

Knowing that I have faults that I can't fix should ensure that I find some humility. In fellowship, we see the face of God. The graced opportunities that only arise in community, despite the flaws in *every* community. So in this state where I know I need help, it comes, slowly. Often in the guise of others on my journey that strengthen, challenge and guide me to be the best version of myself. But none of that can happen if I am closed off and think I have all of the answers. May I be open to all that I might receive.

11 November

*Eighth step: Made a list of all persons we had harmed,
and became willing to make amends to them all.*

Rather than my acknowledgment of my failings just being a thought experiment, I need to prepare to enact my plan. And preparations are important. Making lists prompts further thinking and people/situations I had forgotten may be brought to mind. In terms of making amends, some will be more challenging than others. Money can be repaid but mending damaged relationships require time and love… and grace. Partners who have been cheated on; long time friends cut out; parents taken for granted. Like gardening, patience is required. And the best harvests are achieved with preparation.

12 November

*So if I, your Lord and Teacher, have washed your feet,
you also ought to wash one another's feet. (John 13:14)*

In the 21st century, such an expression is a figure of speech whereas at the time of Jesus this was an everyday occurrence typically done by a slave. For us, it is about being of service and following the example of Jesus. Whether we think of today or the past, there are those in one form of leadership or another who have followed this advice – and those who haven't. Any organisation including a church that has servant leaders will be healthy and any malaise will stem back to the absence of servant leaders. When I try to be a servant leader, wondrous things happen!

13 November

We journey together.
Our task
For those in our care
Is to point the way.
This can be a daunting prospect
Through our own stumbles
Or uncertainty.
We must remember
The focus is Love
The One who is love
Who loved each of us
Into being.
If we journey
With love
In love
Attending to each image of Love
We find that
The journey
And destination
Are One

14 November

The entire material universe speaks of God's love, his boundless affection for us. Soil, water, mountains: everything is, as it were, a caress of God. (Pope Francis, Laudato Sí, 84)

God is love (1 John 4:8) and so God's actions express love. God loves humanity and so God's creation expresses God's love for humanity – but also for life itself. Creation as a whole *is good*. There is a harmony and order to life that has been spoken of by priests, seers and poets for centuries. It is little wonder that people speak of the need to be in/with nature – to bring peace, to be made whole. And humanity would thwart its own innate urges through greed and despoil God's gift. I must examine my actions to ensure that I am in balance with God's creation.

15 November　　　　*Helene de Chappotin*

We must always contribute to the spirit of charity and peace; may we ourselves never wound charity by word or deed. (Helene de Chappotin)

This sets the bar high, but it reminds us of our impact. What we each do creates ripples. People in our communities notice what we say and what we do – my language, my tone, how I am with others, my warmth (or its lack). 'Charity' can also be translated as 'self-sacrificing love'. For a community to be truly effective and functional, self-sacrificing love must be plentiful.

This adds to a sense of peace. If people are upset about the way they or others have been spoken to or treated, this diminishes peace. Contributing to a 'spirit of charity and peace' builds community – and brings God's reign closer.

16 November

From panoramic vistas to the tiniest living form, nature is a constant source of wonder and awe. It is also a continuing revelation of the divine. (Pastoral letter of Canadian Bishops, 2003, quoted in Pope Francis, Laudato Sí, *85)*

Wonder and awe is a gift of the Holy Spirit. Wonder and awe allow me to perceive that God is at work in the world. That can be seen on a micro level through sub-atomic particles and tiny organisms. It can also be seen on the macro level in the grandeur of scenery or the extraordinary forces at work in a storm. Whether order or chaos, there is a harmony that is being wrought in it all that we need to grasp – as much as possible. In the busyness of each day, do I take time to notice God's handiwork around me? Such an activity will refresh and sustain me.

17 November

I give you a new commandment, that you love one another. Just as I have loved you, you also should love one another. (John 13:34)

Self-sacrificing love is costly but reaps wonderful rewards – ask a parent. But the example that Jesus gave was his giving unto death. That's a big ask. As challenging as this commandment is, it is what was needed to overcome the hurdles that the early church faced. Not only that, this form of giving is a death to ego which ensures that I am following God's plan – that of love – not my own plan. And by ensuring that ego is not *sine qua non* I am more concerned about others and so am more likely to build right relationships and justice.

18 November

Ninth step: Made direct amends to such people wherever possible, except when to do so would injure them or others.

It is one matter to have the intention to fix things, it is even more important to follow through, to do what you've said you will do. A key phrase is 'direct amends'. This means I'm dealing with the person(s) in person; not via phone, email or text. Making amends looks different in different situations. In some circumstances, it could prove quite lengthy – but it is important to make amends. So that I can behave in a way that is truly me.

The second clause is significant. It acknowledges that it is not just about *me*. In a particular circumstance, I could open old wounds that are better left in an effort to get rid of my feeling of guilt. Am I mindful of my impact upon my relationships?

19 November

I give you a new commandment, that you love one another. Just as I have loved you, you also should love one another. (John 13:34)

We are each love made flesh. Not just the loving act that created me and brought me into the world. All along the way of my development and growth I have been shaped by the love that has been showered on me – by my parents, by my family, by my friends, by my partner, by my children. Who I am in a very real way is a consequence of the love that I have received – from God and each other person along my life's journey. Yet, love is also meant to be given. So I become who I truly am by *giving* love in all its forms to those in my life – but especially self-sacrificing love – that stretches me and helps me to grow. Love has seven billion faces in the world. I am a *unique* incarnation of love so my contribution is to be myself.

20 *November*

Tenth step: Continued to take personal inventory and when we were wrong promptly admitted it.

It is easy to be lulled into a false sense of security: 'I got this!' The human capacity for self-delusion is immense and seen in addicts. Recovery must be active and sustained – or I revert to old patterns of behaviour. How am I going today? This week? Am I being true to myself? To everyone and everything I hold dear? When I stuff up, as I inevitably will, I admit my mistake, mend any relationship harmed and keep moving. This kind of vigilance keeps me grounded. It allows me to see how far I have come and how far I have to go – but there is the joy of needing the help of others to get there.

21 *November*

I am the true vine. (John 15:1)

As humans we crave connection. Depending upon the circumstances we can choose our friends well... or poorly. A vine requires all of its parts to do their job individually *and* work together which is the only way it will bear good fruit. Especially today, communities can be very 'loose'; a bit light on working together. So if we each follow Jesus and 'dial down' our egos, we are more truly connected. This is when extraordinary and beautiful things happen!

22 November

Bathed
In
Golden sunshine
At 6.15am
Is a
Wondrous gift
To start my day
It beats the heck
Out of the
Cold and dark
And ensuing
Existential questions

Summer is almost
Upon us
With its promise
Of sunshine
And warmth
May my heart
Remain open

23 November

Jesus said to him, 'I am the way, and the truth and the life'. (John 14:6)

Do you want to know how to live? Live like Jesus – that is 'the way'. Which means a life of caring for those on the margins, loving others unconditionally, building relationships through compassion, staying on track through prayer and contemplation. Another understanding of the Greek word that is translated as 'truth' is 'well foundedness'. Living as Jesus did is also 'well founded'. It brings a deep happiness, peace and joy. This way of living speaks to the truth of the human condition. Living this way gives life – not just for me but to everyone around me.

24 November

Eleventh step: Sought through prayer and meditation to improve our conscious contact with God, as we understood God, praying only for knowledge of God's will for us and the power to carry that out.

It is easy for me to think I'm doing the right thing. Others can also tell me so. But prayer and contemplation will ground me in God. That which is ego-driven recoils from resting in God's loving gaze. In prayer and contemplation I am truly myself and God loves me as I am. When a group that is looking to move forward together harnesses this, extraordinary things can happen. Such a community respects the gifts of each person and utilises them to build the community – and delights in doing so. It is not a game, nor a race. There will be obstacles that can be overcome – together.

25 November

This place is so beautiful
So peaceful
I needed this
More than I could say

As I get ready to leave
I want to cram in
Every last piece of peace
I can

But I am so grateful for this opportunity
To slow down
And imbibe
The unique combination
Of sun and clouds
Birds and trees
And natural beauty
Whose endpoint is peace
That is Assisi

26 November

This contemplation of creation allows us to discover
in each thing a teaching which God wishes to hand on
to us (Pope Francis, Laudato Sí, 85)

'Contemplation of creation' is a phrase that carries a lot as there are so many layers; as individual creatures or facets, their interaction and then more broadly as a system. Animate and inanimate. It is easy to spend so much time looking at clouds in the sky OR a view of the ocean OR sitting in a park OR... The teaching could be the extraordinary beauty and complexity that requires no human intervention (and is better off without it). The teaching could be the peace or rejuvenation or harmony to be gained. Am I making opportunities to be taught by God?

27 November

Twelfth step: Having had a spiritual awakening as
a result of these steps, we tried to carry this message
to addicts, and to practise these principles in all our
affairs.

Such a spiritual awakening affects different people in diverse ways. One way might be the sense of seeing the world as if for the first time – and everything is sweet! Through accepting God's love, I am not judging myself. Now that I am in recovery, I seek connection with others. Some carry the message to other addicts quietly; others with more gusto. The spiritual awakening increases my compassion for those I can see who are in a different spot of the journey I have been on. I can see them wrestling in the dark. I also know I can't save them – just be there for them. By practising these principles, I am conscious of my failings. I am conscious of my impact upon relationships. And I am constantly looking to be grounded in God. This is the path towards wholeness and holiness – for anyone.

28 November

You are my friends if you do what I command you.
(John 15:14)

It could be seen as a literary device that the commandment to love is repeated. It could also be an understanding of the need for humans to have a message repeated so that it sinks in! Jesus' relationship with the Twelve (who are not called 'apostles' in John) has been one of teacher and students. In this Last Discourse, Jesus is setting them up for his departure. By calling them 'friends', he is putting them on a more level footing (as far-fetched as that may seem!). Friends have shared expectations. So the Twelve can prove their level footing with Jesus through self-sacrificing love – unto death. Sets the bar high...

29 November

*We fail to see that some are mired in desperate and
degrading poverty, with no way out, while others
have not the faintest idea of what to do with their
possessions, vainly showing off their supposed
superiority and leaving behind them so much waste
which, if it were the case everywhere, would destroy
the planet. (Pope Francis,* Laudato Sí, *90)*

Many people in developed countries live lives that are
oblivious to their *real* cost; the cost that is paid by damage
to the environment; the cost that is paid by those who
can least afford it. Partly, this is fuelled by an insecurity
that needs to flaunt possessions and/or status. It is also
fuelled by 'Holy Spirit atheism' – God is not truly at work
in the world and I can do as I please. What I must do is
concern myself with the plank in my own eye, rather
than the speck in my sister's eye. Thus I need to examine
my actions and lifestyle to minimise my impact upon
people and planet.

30 November

I believe in one Lord Jesus Christ,
the Only Begotten Son of God,
born of the Father before all ages. (Nicene Creed)

The first four and a half centuries of the Church's existence was spent grappling and fighting about who Jesus was and how (or if) he was divine. That length of time with its accumulated experience and wisdom were needed to discern an appropriately rich answer. In the end, it was decided that Jesus of Nazareth was also divine and pre-existent with God. This aligns with the scriptural witness in each of the Gospels. The 'formula' may have been settled but today each person still needs to wrestle with the meaning for *them*. Will my faith help me to live in a wholehearted and life-giving way?

DECEMBER

1 December

Beware, keep alert; for you do not know when the time will come. (Mark 13:33)

We arrive again at Advent. We anticipate Christmas. This might cause excitement, anxiety...or a little of both. This passage shows an awareness of human nature. We can be so busy making plans that we forget to live in *this* moment. We fail to ask: what's going on? In so doing we can miss the joy and pain of our fellow human beings - the stuff of life. If we pay even closer attention, this is where God is at work - the Love weaving the tapestry of the universe.

So our task is to learn to be awake and aware. Aware of God at work in our lives: through prayer, through life's events, through the love of family and friends. Jesus Christ is the fullness of the Incarnation but like a spiritual Big Bang, the Love continues to saturate us with its radiance. In the words of Michael Leunig: 'love is always born'.

2 December

I believe in the Holy Spirit, the Lord, the giver of life,
who proceeds from the Father and the Son,
who with the Father and the Son is adored and
glorified,
who has spoken through the prophets. (Nicene Creed)

While the Holy Spirit is one of the three persons (or ways that humans perceive God), there is one God. Since God loves God's creation in all its forms, it only makes sense that God would continually be at work in the world. The Holy Spirit is at work in the world giving life and bringing things to fullness. Humans go on a tangent easily and so need guidance. This has happened formally through the prophets but there are many people who have sincerely engaged in ministry of one form or another whose heart and hands have been guided by the Holy Spirit – for the good of community. When one is engaged in ministry, it is better to attribute all to the Holy Spirit rather than be seduced by one's ego.

3 December

Again Peter denied it, and at that moment the cock crowed. (John 18:27)

Peter denies Jesus – but this is not a 'one-off' accident. He has had a chance to 'get it right'. He denies Jesus three times. This is Peter, head of the Twelve. The person who came to be known, in retrospect, as the first pope, the first bishop of Rome. This is telling for a number of reasons. If a person with the status in the church that Peter had can get it wrong (so spectacularly!), then it's OK for others to make mistakes too. What it also does is demonstrate the fallibility of church leaders. Would that this was kept in mind throughout the 2000 year history of Christianity! History, including very recent events, has proved the power of this passage. May we remember this lesson of the fallibility of church leaders – always!

4 December

I sit
Staring
At this salve
Timeless wonder
Of sea, sky and light
Of waves rolling and lapping

As day follows day
The scene's colours
Morph
Through a thousand
Greys and blues
Each unique
Precious
Stunning

Peace-giver
Medicine
To heal
Life's cares

5 December

Prepare the way of the Lord,
make his paths straight. (Mark 1:3)

Advent is where we take stock of our lives in preparation for the coming of Christ at Christmas. In our preparations, are we ensuring that those on the outer are included in our communities? Are we ensuring that their needs are met? Am I ensuring that I treat everyone around me with love and compassion? It is easy to get caught up in life's twists and turns. Am I being straightforward with others – no double agendas? Am I a person of integrity?

6 December

Faithfulness has disappeared;
the word itself is banished from their speech.
(Jeremiah 7:28)

One might get this sense in the middle of an election campaign: 'Does anyone speak the truth?' 'Who can I trust?' Instead, let's look inward: in what ways am I faithful and trustworthy? A point of distinction for me has been to discern whether I am motivated by a desire to look good in someone's eyes or I am motivated to do what is right. And if I am still long enough, I get the prompt to do what is right. The choice is rarely between good and bad; it might be between good and better. But I need to be still. I need to make time to be still and listen. God will show me the way.

7 December

It is clearly inconsistent to combat trafficking in endangered species while remaining completely indifferent to human trafficking, unconcerned about the poor, or undertaking to destroy another human being deemed unwanted. (Pope Francis, Laudato Sí, 91)

We return to the connection between environmental and social justice issues. I need to see the big picture and not focus on one to the exclusion of the other. Treating *God's* creation as an item for my profit is wrong. It is wrong to sell wildlife or people for profit. Doing so is to be deaf to what God can teach me from each part of creation. As a consumer I can make choices about shopping ethically and thus not supporting trafficking of any sort. This consumer pressure yields results slowly but effectively.

8 December

Abraham replied, 'They have Moses and the prophets; they should listen to them'. He said, 'No, father Abraham; but if someone goes to them from the dead, they will repent'. He said to him, 'If they do not listen to Moses and the prophets, neither will they be convinced even if someone rises from the dead'. (Luke 16:29-31)

'You can lead a horse to water but you can't make it drink.' No matter how obvious something is, people still make a choice. This is especially true when it comes to matters of faith. It also doesn't matter how old someone is. Faith must be a personal choice or assent. Being brought up in the faith can be very helpful, but at some point each person who has been presented with the faith option through family, friends, school or work *must* make a personal choice: I believe... or not. What one person finds convincing, another finds limp. I think example works best. What do you think?

9 *December*

Another working day
Ends
The summer heat makes me
Especially grateful
That it is over.

Dark clouds
Begin to brood
Until a summer deluge
Descends
With its rain, hail and wind

In a brief cessation
Of hostilities
The clouds part
To reveal
Shafts of sunlight
Cascading their promise

10 *December*

He has brought down the powerful from their
thrones, and lifted up the lowly. (Luke 1:52)

This verse continues Mary's statement of faith in God. Like its Old Testament counterpart, Hannah's canticle in 1 Samuel 2, Mary's faith is remarkable. The *Magnificat* also looks forward to the great overturning that happens through Jesus outlined in this Gospel. What is the context? The Jewish people are diminished, conquered by Rome. Where is hope? There is faith in a salvation in *this* life. The rich and powerful will get their comeuppance and, again like the Old Testament, the poor, the widow and the stranger will be cared for.

This passage resonates with our sense of justice. We must try to grasp Mary's faith that God will work in the hearts of people to ensure that, however slowly, those in need are taken care of. And, that it starts with me.

11 *December*

All of those who believed were of one heart and soul.
(Acts 4:32)

What a joyous situation! Groups of humans can be like this but there can also be pockets of people looking to move in a different direction – and not necessarily out of any negative motives. In a world that promotes the individual (essentially as a marketing tool and political pacifier), how can I be united with others without being a sheep? Individual gifts are celebrated in the body of Christ but it is only *in community* that my gifts come to fullness. I have my part to play in community guided by God through prayer and contemplation.

12 December

Those who do what is true come to the light, so that it may be clearly seen that their deeds have been done in God. (John 3:21)

Over my lifetime, I have noticed people looking over their shoulders if they do not want to be seen – some body language cues are shared. If I lie constantly, I need to remember my lies otherwise I will be caught out. I am dodging the light. In the light, it is easy to see; and if I remain in the light, I can see and be seen. I have nothing to hide. All our words about God fall short but light is a powerful metaphor for God who is truth, love, compassion and so much more. If I am searching for truth, love and compassion, I will eventually emerge from the shadows and revel in the light of God rather than be distracted by the darkness of my own selfish ends.

13 December

Everything is related, and we human beings are united as brothers and sisters on a wonderful pilgrimage, woven together by the love God has for each of his creatures and which also unites us in fond affection with brother sun, sister moon, brother river and mother earth. (Pope Francis, Laudato Sí, 92)

Part of God's message of love in creation is the wonder of the variety of connections between living and non-living things. Seeing our journey of life as a pilgrimage is transformative. A pilgrimage is a contemplative experience rather than just a series of events or a passing of time. A pilgrimage is a way to more deeply discern God's hand in my life. As I rise to the challenge of learning God's message of love in each part of creation, that is best done in the contemplative space that is part of the pilgrimage. I need to grasp opportunities to foster such a contemplative space, at least daily.

14 December

You are who you are in the eyes of God, nothing more
and nothing less. (St Francis of Assisi)

To be able to see things clearly is a helpful attribute.
This is all the more true when it comes to seeing myself.
I have so many filters and 'distortions' in the mirror
so that I do not always see myself truly. What might
Francis mean? I need to be able to see the giftedness and
inherent goodness and dignity that have been placed in
me by God. If I truly see that, I cannot despise myself
even though I may not always live up to my ideals. The
'nothing more' part is if I consider myself 'above' others
or focus on my status or money or achievements. If I see
myself truly and know my true worth, I am able to be
in relationship with others as I am on the same level as
them. It is in the relationships of the body of Christ that
I find my salvation from isolation and loneliness and
that I glimpse God's reign... and God's face in the faces
of those around me.

15 December

For Robert – friend and former student. Gone too soon

Bright light
Who brought laughter
And joy and love
Flamed out
Too soon
Few knew
The extent
Of the darkness
With which you wrestled
For so long

As I travel
Through the land of beauty
In which you grew
I struggle to believe
Your passing

May you now feel and know
The love
From your partner
And family
And friends.
May you be bathed
In laughter
And joy
And colour
And peace
Now

16 December

He who saw this has testified so that you also may
believe. His testimony is true, and he knows that he
tells the truth. (John 19:35)

The life, death and resurrection of Jesus is one heck of a
story. While it is a faith story and less concerned about
history, the evangelist wished to establish *the truth* of the
story of Jesus – thus the need for eyewitness verification.
Yet the point of the facts is to believe in Jesus. We live at a
time when scientific truth seems to override everything.
Yet we know the truth, the power of the less tangible –
like love. How do we measure love? We *know* it is real
and we know how life is impoverished without it. Love,
no matter its form, enriches life and helps us to feel
whole and connected. We believe that God is present
in everyone and everything. We also believe that God is
love. All make sense?

17 December

Do not be upset by others' failings 'because such anger and annoyance will make it difficult to be charitable'. (Rule of St Francis of Assisi)

Like me, you may have heard someone say: 'they made me do it'. While understandable in children, such a statement abrogates personal responsibility. As an adult I make choices – whether I am conscious of them or not. I have made a choice of faith, since no one can force faith upon me. I am God's heart and hands, acting with love for all in my life – as nearly as I can. However, most of these obstacles for my living the Gospel are *in me* such as my need for the esteem of others or of control. So what I must do, over time, is build a bridge over myself so that I can be charitable to everyone around me. Sound like a life's work?

18 December

Jesus said to her, 'Mary!' She turned and said to him in Hebrew, 'Rabbouni!' (which means Teacher). (John 20:16)

The person who knows me by name has a special connection with me. It is this personal connection that Jesus uses to shine a light in Mary Magdalene's darkness – a darkness caused by Mary thinking that Jesus' death was the end. Mary responds in a personal way, calling Jesus 'teacher' rather than 'Lord'. What might this passage be saying? When I am in darkness (of some sort or another), it is not creedal statements that will reach me – rather the God who knows my name and loves me into life. And we should employ the same love with those in need...

19 December

You can show your love to others by not wishing that they should be better Christians. (St Francis of Assisi)

Wishing others to be better could be seen as condescending. A sub-text being they should be 'as good as me'. Such an attitude is controlling not loving. Rather, a loving attitude is to admit *my* faults and failings (by worrying about the plank in own eye not the speck in the eye of another) and wish them well on their faith journey. A loving attitude could be based in my ignorance of another. *Their* gifts and the part they could (or do) play in the body of Christ might have nothing to do with me. The greatness of the body of Christ is when each of us plays our part *for* the community rather than an ego-driven agenda. As Christians *we* come undone when we ignore that we are each daughters and sons of God – and so equal.

20 *December*

He has filled the hungry with good things,
and sent the rich away empty. (Luke 1:53)

Such ideas continue to be counter-cultural. The rich and powerful make the rules. There are many rationalisations for greed. Fairness and justice is about building right relationships, i.e. bringing God's reign closer. Thus this passage is about overturning human logic and reminding us of what will make us whole and holy.

The person of faith, with the Scriptures (Old and New Testament) as template, has the whole community as their focus since we need *everyone* (each making their unique contribution) to be saved.

21 *December*

If I tell them, they will consider me a fool; if I am
silent, I cannot escape my conscience. (Francis of
Assisi, before warning Christian Crusaders)

Francis captures the heart of an ethical crisis. Who wins – my desire for esteem or my integrity? I live and work with people every day – my relationships are very important. Potentially jeopardising those relationships is no small step. Yet, if I do not have integrity, who am I? My experience has taught me the inestimable value of integrity. When all is said and done, I need to look in the mirror and live with myself. Somehow, Francis negotiated a path forward, despite flying in the face of papal and temporal power. In my life, I know that truth does not always win but can I ignore my conscience?

22 *December*

Morning
Warmed by northerlies
Timeless and primeval
Meeting
Of sand, sea and sky

Wading
Through shin-deep
Clear water.
Brooding clouds above
Ripple marks
And worm trails
Beneath my feet.
Seagulls sitting
On their rock

In this liminal space
Each breath
Each step
Sings praise
To the One
Who made it all.

23 December

*Looking at the stars, Francis said: 'If these are the
creatures, what must the creator be like?' (Quoted by
Richard Rohr in Eager to Love, The alternative way
of Francis of Assisi)*

Faith can be a slippery thing. It is not faith if I need proof
but what can bolster my faith if I cannot perceive it?
Francis did so much more than 'love the animals' yet this
quote indicates the solace and inspiration he received
from observing and interacting with God's creation.
God's creation in all its varied forms is around me
every day. I can ponder and wonder at a living creature
fossilised and thus preserved for millions of years. I can
delight in the delicate rainbow refraction of light. I can
marvel at the trees and grasses that generate their own
food through photosynthesis and give off oxygen that I
breathe not to mention that they are food and home for
other creatures. The subtlety and complexity of it all. O
God, how great you are!

24 December

*A guru asked his disciples how they could tell when
the night had ended and day begun. One said, 'When
you see an animal in the distance and can tell whether
it is a cow or a horse'. 'No', said the guru. 'When you
look at a tree in the distance and can tell if it is a neem
tree or a mango tree.' 'Wrong again', said the guru.
'Well, then, what is it?' asked the disciples.
'When you look into the face of any man and
recognise your brother in him: when you look into the
face of any woman and recognise in her your sister. If
you cannot do this, no matter what time it is by the
sun it is still night.' (Anthony de Mello,* Prayer of
the Frog, *p. 227).*

At Christmas, we celebrate Emmanuel, God-with-us.
How can we recognise God with us if 'it is still night'?
As I look around today, I see those whose lives are lived
in the light – who recognise each person as their sister
or brother. I also see those whose lives are more in
shadow. Christmas reminds us that all is not as it could
be. However, Christmas also reminds us where we are
headed and God's grace will guide us.

25 December

Mary will bear a son, and you are to name him
Jesus, for he will save his people from their sins.
(Matthew 1:21)

Christmas gathers up so many memories and so many feelings – and not all of them are happy. It can be an acutely painful time for some as the pain of absence stands in stark contrast to the joy of others. Christmas is the celebration of God-with-us, incarnate love. And as much as love swells our hearts, love can also wound – ask any parent. We put so much on one day – impossibly high expectations – but love should be for every day. If 25 December doesn't go to plan, there are 364 other days to express our love in tangible ways. Expressions of love to our nearest and dearest but also expressions of Love whether in prayer, delight in God's creation or care for those in need. And be open to how Love can teach you – every day.

26 December

Look, the virgin shall conceive and bear a son,
and they shall name him Emmanuel,
which means, 'God is with us.' (Matthew 1:23)

As much as we like to ponder matters, as humans, at times we need the concrete to learn or really grasp a point. The Hebrew Scriptures and the New Testament speak of God's love for us. At Christmas, we celebrate the Incarnation: God-with-us/Emmanuel – love made flesh. This is the concrete example that we humans need. This is what love looks like. Jesus and Mary live out what love looks like. They live out the unique and precious ways that Love can guide and shape us.

Gathering at Christmas with our family and friends, let us give thanks for the love that we share which binds us. This same love that can help us to lift the veil from our eyes and see that we are *all* one. This precious Christmas gift needs to be savoured each and every day.

27 December

Busy?
Bored?
Time *is* perception
Filled with work or duties
Days whizz past

Summer holidays
Time *stretches*
Days pass
Yet seem slower
Until they end.
... and we turn around
And mourn their loss

28 December

*Jesus answered them, 'This is the work of God, that
you believe in him whom he has sent'. (John 6:29)*

What does it mean to believe in Jesus? For some it has
been a matter of intellectual assent yet doesn't really
affect their living. For John the use of the verb implies
action – how am I *living* that I believe in Jesus? Am I
engaged in prayer and contemplation to be guided by
God? Do I read the Bible to aid my discernment? We
are saved in and for community. Are my relationships
marked by respect, compassion and empathy? Do I help
those in need, near and far? Part of the 'work of God' is
to show us that we are *one* – sisters and brothers of the
Father who loved each of us into life. Do my words and
actions divide or unite?

29 December

Walking on the beach
My love beside me
Ben Harper's sweet slide
In my head
Breeze clears out
The summer heat
Dogs racing for the ball
Sky full of clouds
Of different shapes
Makes the sea
Look majestically leaden
Sunshine
Makes the ochre cliffs
Glow
Waves rolling to shore
In the distance
Rain is falling
This new day

30 *December*

But there are also many other things that Jesus did;
if every one of them were written down, I suppose
that the world itself could not contain the books that
would be written. (John 21:25)

The Gospel is *not* a history; it is a faith document. Thus selections were made about what to include. If we are to focus on the three-year public ministry of Jesus – a lot could be written. Another point is that the life of Jesus created ripples that spread and affected an even greater number of people, e.g. the woman at the well (John 4:1-42). If I were to write my own faith story, whom would I include? What people and events have shaped me? How has my faith story created ripples? Who and how have others been affected?

31 December

A year comes to a close
A new one beckons
Nothing changes
It's another day
And yet it is a liminal space

This is not 'groundhog day'
This is an opportunity
To choose
Be intentional
About my relationships
About my actions
About focusing on love
As that which binds
Everything

Choose gospel values
And make heaven real
Each day

Lightning Source UK Ltd.
Milton Keynes UK
UKHW041452281220
375896UK00001B/14

9 780648 804499